Palo Alto City Library

The individual borrower is responsible for all library material borrowed on his card.

Charges as determined by the CITY OF PALO ALTO will be assessed for each overdue item.

Damaged or non-returned property will be billed to the individual borrower by the CITY OF PALO ALTO.

Instant Beauty

The Complete Way to Perfect Makeup

by **PABLO MANZONI**
of **Elizabeth Arden**

Introduction by *Diana Vreeland*
Drawings by *John Ansado*

SIMON AND SCHUSTER
NEW YORK

Designed by Elizabeth Woll
Manufactured in the United States of America

1   2   3   4   5   6   7   8   9   10

Library of Congress Cataloging in Publication Data

Pablo, 1939–
  Instant beauty.

  Includes index.
  1. Beauty, Personal. 2. Cosmetics. I. Title.
RA778.P2   646.7′26   77-27859

ISBN 0-671-22555-3

Acknowledgment

I would particularly like to thank my co-author, Rochelle Larkin, without whom this book might not have been possible. It was with infinite pleasure that I realized how, in the course of working together, we became such good friends, as Rochelle gave me much more than she can ever know.

This book is dedicated to ALL women . . . with the most sincere wish that my simple philosophy of being oneself at one's best will encourage them to consider my approach that "less is better"— a simple rule that has taken .the most interesting beauties a lifetime to learn

Contents

Introduction

Pablo is a charming, talented artist whom I have known for years. He is always filled with enthusiasm and a great sense of fun, but seriousness and thoroughness are at the base of everything he loves and undertakes.

In writing this book, he has brought to the reader both his flair and his incredible understanding of a woman's face and her potential for real beauty. He has put an emphasis on creating natural, believeable looks with ease, simplicity and using a minimum of makeup items. Just take a look at the chapter titles to see that the limited time of the busy woman is something he understands well. He has arranged five-, ten- and twenty-minute makeup routines that are simplicity itself and work miraculously. He, of course, would never neglect skin care, as no makeup can really be put over anything but a perfect base. For this reason he has included a complete care regimen for each skin type.

Pablo is as concerned with economy as he is with time and elegance. He tells the reader that she need have no more than one or two lipsticks, one basic foundation and that a box of powder should last for years. With the help of an inexpensive tool such as the sponge, she can achieve tremendous results that are at once beautiful and natural and save time in the process. And yet, along with economy, there are many suggestions for pampering and self-indulgence, which all women love—you know what luxury does to bring a marvelous sparkle to a woman's eyes.

The book is written in a flowing, conversational voice. Pablo takes a totally honest approach, for he is committed to helping the American woman understand and appreciate herself. He has the talent for recognizing the potential and beauty of each face and he shares this knowledge with the reader.

Pablo believes that one of the secrets to attaining great beauty is self-acceptance. This leads to the greatest treasure—individualism and a personal style.

Pablo wants every woman to develop her natural potential. Beauty as perfection in features is not important to him. He believes that every intelligent woman can, through immaculate, painstaking grooming, even turn her flaws into assets.

Pablo believes that the best use of one's bone structure is important; having great bones is like having money in the bank. He talks, as well, of the importance of eye makeup, which creates a wordless message communicated with glamour, totally believeable glamour. As always, it is not the amount, but the proper application that creates the look.

Included in the book is a chapter on some of the most famous and interesting faces of our time with candid photographs; Pablo's approach to them is unique and his description of ideal makeup for them is sheer artistry.

Pablo has lived up to the promise of the book making it wonderfully concise and clear. It is a superb opportunity for every woman to learn that *simplicity* is the key to both doing what she wants to do and doing it well.

Diana Vreeland

Preface

A poet once wrote, "Beauty is truth, truth beauty." He was probably right, but impractical, as poets usually are.

The standards of female beauty have changed greatly since his time and have become much more exciting. The concepts of perfection, of only one certain look being correct, of slavish imitation of some imagined ideal are gone. What has replaced them in the world of fashion and beauty are concepts of individual freedom that allow every woman to be herself—her best self.

Every woman has an inborn sense of beauty she should strive to develop to its fullest. She has a great potential for beauty: her face, her clothes, her poise and charm all come together to create a whole. We carry this beauty within ourselves, we convey it to others, we learn to appreciate the beauty that is all around us.

I see the beauty in thousands of women each year as I travel across the country, and I see women as no one else does. At the center of my philosophy of beauty is the tenet that every woman is uniquely, individually beautiful. I do not believe that a beautiful woman is a woman with a perfect face; it is distinctive features, which some women look on as "flaws," that make each face interesting. I teach a woman to play up, not play down, her special deviations. They exist to be turned to her advantage; they make her chic and memorable. In this post-sixties era we are all finally beginning to realize that character adds more to a face than even lipstick or eye color can.

There was a time, at the start of this century, when today's beauties—women like Barbra Streisand, Karen Black, Lauren Hutton—wouldn't have stood a chance. Ironically, it was the director whose many innovations turned moviemaking into an art form, D. W. Griffith, who was responsible for some of the most clichéd ideas on women and female beauty.

"We pick the little women," he is quoted as having said, "because the world loves youth, and all its wistful sweetness . . . Youth with its dreams and sweetness, youth with its romance and adventure . . ." Thus the Griffith actresses were all small, young and slim, and they set the standard for screen beauty and for the vast audience as well. For decades the only face thought to be photogenic was perfectly oval-shaped, with almond-shaped eyes framed in long lashes, rosebud lips, a tiny, straight or turned-up nose, and long hair, crimped, curled, waved.

Though movies still accent youth, as does advertising in magazines, newspapers and television, the movies have at least conceded the value of nonconformity in looks.

Now that women are liberated and free to be attractive each in her own way, we have to approach makeup in a new way too. A woman wears makeup; makeup does not wear the woman. It enhances the face, it doesn't hide it. This is perhaps the most difficult concept for most women to grasp.

Generally I believe that less makeup is better than more. The whole idea of makeup is to make you look and feel like yourself at your very best. Please notice that I said feel as well as look your best. Your innermost feelings about yourself, your life and the world you live in all influence the way you approach makeup, and so we will explore those areas too. Throughout my book I want to tell you about all the factors that affect the way you look, how your looks affect those around you, and the constant interplay. I want to share with you all that I have seen, experienced and learned from my thousands of clients in almost every major city across the United States.

As you read, you will find yourself positively reconsidering your approach to makeup, putting thought into every touch of your face even before you learn any new techniques or start using colors. And improvement will be immediate, I promise.

As you begin to understand and use my methods of makeup and skin-care application you will find yourself looking better than you thought you ever could, using fewer cosmetics than you're using now, and using them more simply and easily. As you become more of an expert about yourself you may even be spending less time in front of your makeup mirror—as you will see, five minutes will be enough to make you look stunning without looking made-up.

At the same time, I expect that many of my readers will be putting more thought into the care of their faces than they're used to. Everything from air pollution to air conditioning seems to take its toll on your face; the woman who wants to look her best today (and for years to come) has to invest time in a good, strict skin-care program—attention that wasn't needed by generations of women who lived in simpler times.

Happily, today's beauty aids are far more advanced than the limited and seldom effective preparations of your grandmother's and even your mother's day. There is help for every type of skin problem that exists. Medical and scientific research in cosmetics and makeup is a vast field of technology, and every woman is a beneficiary.

When I talk about makeup I must also talk about style and its importance. Though I am a makeup artist, I look at the complete woman. The beauty in her face should continue throughout her whole person; it mustn't stop at her neck. It is my hope that every woman will find her own style, for indeed every woman has one, but it must be nurtured and developed. It is what makes each of us, men included, a unique and special person.

To be honest, I would have to say that the sense of style is much more highly developed in European women in all walks of life than it is here. In Europe a woman is much less afraid of being an individual, more likely to dress and make up as her own sense of self-assurance prompts her, and look marvelous doing it. A woman who achieves a strong sense of herself can acquire a strong sense of fashion, one she won't be willing to reject for the newest color or the latest hemlines. She doesn't fall prey to fads in fashion that are frequently more suitable for her teenage daughter and often mass-produced and sold with no thought to individual suitability. This is usually true of makeup as well, and just as you acquire your own style and look in fashion, you acquire a look with makeup, one that shouldn't be forgotten with the appearance of a new shade or consistency of foundation, for example.

I don't believe that failure to adopt a particular look, no matter how strong a fashion statement it makes at the moment, makes a chic woman unchic. Second, I don't believe that a woman should ever wear something that is unbecoming to her. If you feel strongly about being part of the current trend, buy a pair of gloves, a scarf, a piece of jewelry that has the new look, an accessory that will dramatize rather than dominate.

Accessories are important not only because they are the way out of conformity, a means of wearing just a touch of fashion, but because they are a way of expressing yourself, your awareness, and for enhancing your best features—a new belt for a slim waistline, for instance.

Makeup, too, can be a new means of achieving individuality. But it must be considered in its total context; you can't isolate it from the rest of you. Total harmony is the look you should be striving for, and makeup, the proper makeup, can work so well for you.

I love makeup and the things it can do for a woman. I love the way makeup can light up your eyes. The eyes are the windows of the soul—five hundred years ago a countryman of mine, Leonardo da Vinci, said that. It is still true today. I will show you how to complement your eyes and make them the center of your face. There is an instant magic in wearing pretty makeup—when the instant comes from the product and the magic comes from you.

There is no doubt that makeup is the fastest route to looking more beautiful. A jar, a tube, a bottle—and voilà! a better-looking face than the one that just got out of bed.

The chapters on makeup in minutes will help you develop instant routines for flawless applications; the chapters on specific features and areas of the face will help you select the proper colors and formats for your individuality. Refer to the appropriate chapters concurrently as you perfect your routine—and your looks. Check "The Dressing Table Inventory" at the end of the book to learn about those products you might be unfamiliar with. Everything I've written here is for the sole purpose of putting beauty within your reach as simply and easily as possible.

For the woman who already feels quite beautiful, and is secure about her looks, I have many hints about technique that will be of value, as well as new things to try. It is always a lot of fun for a woman to experiment with cosmetics, and the more you do it, the more you learn about them and about yourself. Perhaps something you never thought would work for you looks quite terrific once you try it. And even the most beautiful skin and perfect features need good grooming habits if they are going to stay lovely.

To the youngest readers, to those girls who are just going out into the world of makeup and will have to choose from a bewildering array of preparations, I also offer help. Young faces need less makeup, but it must be chosen and applied every bit as carefully. Young skins have their special problems too, and I will deal with them. Making up is part of growing up, and it can be fun and exciting.

I think that we are ready to get started now. This book will work for you whether you read it straight through or go immediately to what you feel are your special interests. Some sections relate to everyone; others are more specifically addressed. Even if you think a particular area doesn't apply to you, you may still learn something by reading it. Everything here is intended to make you look and feel better than you ever have before.

I'm ready, are *you*?

Part I

MAKEUP IN MINUTES

CHAPTER ONE

The Five-Minute Face

The Five-Minute Makeup Inventory

Sponges: one for applying moisturizer, one for foundation and
rouge; moisten and wring out each thoroughly until barely damp

Cotton swabs and *tissues:* for blending, absorbing and removing excess makeup

Moisturizer: one that is meant to go on under makeup

Foundation: cream or liquid

Rouge: cream or brush-on blusher or both

Eye-shadow pencils: one that compliments your eye color, one in
medium brown, one in medium or skipper blue

Eyeliner and *fine-tipped brush:* preferably sable

Mascara: black brush-on

Lipstick

Lip gloss

Face powder: loose or compact, transparent and colorless

Hand mirror: for side checks and easy eye makeup application

Five minutes in the morning can give you a face that lasts all day.

Five minutes in the evening can create a makeup that keeps on glowing as long as you do.

The knack of applying flawless, believable makeup is something that any woman can learn easily. Part of the trick is in the pre-preparations before you face the mirror. The rest is in the deft application of the easy-to-use cosmetics which will be described completely in this chapter. With a little advance organization, you will soon be able to apply your makeup in much less time than it takes me to tell you about it.

Before you're ready to start, three things must be taken care of so that there will be no time-consuming stops to slow you down: know what you will be wearing, have your dressing table well organized, and take care that your eyebrows have been groomed. The brows should never be tweezed just before you are to make up, because of the redness that occurs; foundation will not always cover it.

If you are well organized, your brows will be perfect, and your dressing table will be completely in order. Everything should always be right at hand, very accessible, and not tucked away in boxes and wrappings. Jars and tubes should always be carefully capped to prevent the contents from drying out and being wasted. If you take just a few seconds to put all your cosmetics in place and to remember where they belong, you'll never have trouble locating any one of them. And when each product is returned to its place after being used, your table will always be in order, and you will be divinely organized.

Your clothes and all accessories should be chosen before you attempt a makeup in minutes. You should feel free to concentrate on your application when you face the mirror without having what-to-wear on your mind. A bright, carefree outlook should be the first on your list of musts.

No matter what the time of day—whether this is a morning or an evening makeup—your face deserves a bright new canvas for the picture you are going to paint on it; a new vision of yourself should always begin clean and healthy. Whether it's to freshen your face in the morning or to remove your old makeup in the evening, you should use cleanser and lotion (as described in the "Healthy Face" section) before you begin, to make your face ready for the new moisturizer.

The best way to apply your moisturizer is to dot it on your forehead, cheeks and chin, and then with long strokes of the sponge draw it smoothly and evenly over the skin. Stroke the sponge gently over your cheeks, toward your temples, always stroking upward, being very careful around the delicate eye area. Your lips and your eyelids too can benefit from this wonderful cosmetic, which I call the foundation's foundation. It is made even more terrific by the use of the sponge, not only for time-saving makeups but for the most elaborate ones as well. Sponges can distribute moisturizer and makeup evenly, picking up excess, which fingers cannot do. I never work without them.

You are ready for your foundation. This is perhaps the most important item in your makeup kit. We will go into much more detail about foundations later, but let me say here that its most important function is that of acting as your second skin.

Thanks to the moisturizer, the application of the foundation is quick and easy. Place a large dot of foundation on your nose, fore-

head, chin and each cheek. Pick up the second sponge and go! Work smoothly and evenly, watching carefully to see that you are creating an even blend of color on your face. Because the foundation contains color pigments and other ingredients, it requires more skillful application than the moisturizer did. Use your fingertips or the edge of the sponge to smoothe out any tiny areas that the full sponge can't reach. Work the color over your lids and lips too. Foundation makes a fabulous base for any other makeup you put over it.

The most important technique in applying foundation, and all other cosmetics, is ensuring that your technique doesn't show. The foundation must be sponged on so smoothly that it seems to become part of the skin itself. Check to see that there is no foundation line around the contour of your jaws and hairline. Make sure that there is none inadvertently clinging to your hair. If you wear your hair short or pulled back, be especially careful of the areas that are exposed. See that the foundation blends in at the top of your neck— this is the most obvious place for demarcation. Turn sideways to your mirror to make sure you have applied the foundation evenly and everywhere.

If you have dark circles under your eyes, cover these with a second coat of the same foundation. Any blemishes or unevenly pigmented areas of the skin can also be concealed by this second coat, which should be applied very lightly with your fingertips and patted into place where it is needed.

Remove any excess carefully with a tissue. Then quickly pat all over with your fingertips, touching to be sure that the color is where it belongs. This patting action is very important. It reassures the skin, which responds incredibly well to your gentle attention. It also affords you an additional check on the eye area and its little hard-to-get-at places. When the amount and the texture of the foundation feels right to you, you can move on to the coloring of the cheeks.

If you have the kind of skin that seems to absorb everything, if your makeup disappears almost immediately after applying it, use a cream rouge. (Later on, you can even brush some extra blusher over it.)

Take the same sponge and apply the rouge from the cheekbones upward. The first application should be made from the front, looking straight into the mirror. Then, when you blend you should look

sideways, making sure you go all the way to the temples, and blend, blend, blend into the foundation so that you cannot tell where one color ends and the other begins.

If you look at the glorious streaks of light in a tropical sunset or the variegations of color on a flower, you'll understand this totally natural effect we're striving for. Colors in nature melt imperceptibly into one another, and this is how the colors of your makeup should work into each other.

At first it may seem as if you're using too much rouge. This is because none of your other features have been made up yet. Later on, after the mouth and eyes have come into the picture, you'll find that the rouge looks less obvious. You may even find yourself wanting to add more.

You might like a touch of rouge at your hairline and on the bridge of your nose. I think this gives a very healthy and alive look. Just a faint hint of color applied with a fingertip. Again touch your face lightly, as you did after applying your foundation.

Now for your eyes! For only the quickest makeup, I favor pencils, the thick crayons that are available today. You can have a lot of fun with these creative playthings and get exciting results, but you should use them very carefully. The eye area is the most delicate on your face, and anything but gentle, tender application of the color pencils can hurt this fragile skin.

Select a color for the lids that complements your eyes. Look down into a hand mirror and stroke the color on, using little light touches. Blend these small strokes with a fingertip or a cotton swab. Make sure that the entire area from the lash line to the crease of the lid is covered, that the color at the outer corner blends into your foundation.

Now look up, straight ahead into the mirror, your chin slightly lowered. Again, with little strokes, color from the outer corner of

the eyelid under to the bottom lashes, midway to the inner corner, for a sweep of color almost completely around the eye—a very flattering look that opens the eye and brightens it.

If you want to make your lashes look fuller with eyeliner, now is the time to use it, not in a straight line but with tiny dots. Looking down into your hand mirror, apply the liner with a fine-tipped sable brush in small dots, going from the outer corner of the upper lid three-quarters of the way toward the inner corner where the lashes actually start. Then, with a fingertip or a swab, smudge the dots, blending one into the next. Don't worry about any unevenness; when your eyes are open, and when your mascara is on, the smudginess will look like the naturally thick roots of your lashes, giving your eyes a pretty, believable, soft look.

The most ideal way to apply mascara is with two hands, one to hold the wand and the other to keep the eyelid taut, which gives you more control. With the middle finger of the free hand gently urge the outer corner of your eye upward, causing it to slant slightly. This will enable you to bring the wand closer to the roots of the lashes and also to get closer to each individual lash. First mascara the top of the upper lashes, from the inner corner out. Then, raising your brows slightly, look straight up into the mirror and mascara the under surface of the upper lashes, coating them thickly with an upward sweep.

In this same pose, do the bottom lashes, stroking sideways as well from time to time, to add fullness. To give mascara time to dry without smudgy mishaps, try not to blink for a few seconds.

When the mascara has dried, take your brown pencil and stroke back and forth in the crease over the bone. After you have accumulated a good amount of color, blend it *all the way* up to the brow, very carefully, very completely, covering the entire area. The immediate effect of this browning is to push back the bone and bring the eyes into greater prominence. It is one of the most beautifying things you can do. (As any stray hairs will pick up the color and retain it, good grooming of the brows is very important; more about that in "A Look at the Eyes.")

If your brows need color for thickness, brush them upwards, and then, with light strokes of your brown pencil, fill them in. The little strokes will simulate little hairs and avoid giving the look of one line

of continuous color. Don't add at the inner corners, just at the arch. Run your finger lightly over the brows to remove any stray or harsh strokes. Always make everything more natural, more you.

By now your mascara is fully dry. A second coat will make the lashes even more lush and sexy, like the rays of a star.

I love to use the medium-blue pencil now to make the eyes even brighter. Carefully line the inner rim of the lower lid with the pencil—the effect is magical. The whites are so white they gleam and the blue color is not even noticeable.

Your lips are next to receive attention. With a lipstick, color your mouth fully, but never go outside or deliberately inside the natural contours of your mouth as this always looks obvious and detracts from your natural beauty.

Add a touch of lip gloss after the lipstick. Twist lips slightly, without actually blotting them, to even out the gloss.

If you like the finishing touch of face powder, powder your nose lightly with either loose or compact powder. If your nose, chin and forehead—the "T" zone—tend to become highlighted and oily during the day, powder that area, leaving lips, eyes and cheeks shiny.

It is now time to reevaluate your rouge. Just a drop more at the tip of the cheekbones and . . . voilà! Finally, if makeup is for daytime, check it in natural light.

Because of all the details I have included, reading this has probably taken you more than five minutes—much more, I am sure, than the actual application will take.

Soon the five-minute makeup will go smoothly and the results will be lovely. Moisturizer, twenty seconds; foundation, one minute; rouge, half a minute; eyes, two minutes; lips, twenty seconds; powder and cheek touch-up, twenty seconds. It is just that simple and easy, just that quick. Remember that, as with anything else, the more you practice, the more proficient you will become.

It's always a good idea to experiment when you have a few minutes. But don't wait to do your first five-minute makeup until you have only five minutes to spare! Learn to do it at leisure so that it is a skill you can use when it's needed.

Your success with the five-minute makeup will depend on the attitude you bring to it. If you are pleased with the results—which you will be if you approach it with a bright outlook and ease—and believe in what you are doing, it will show on your face. If you believe that makeup will work for you, it will. An optimistic attitude will work the wonders—that's a simple fact of psychology which we should all remember. And how you react to yourself will influence how you react to others. If that wasn't important to you, you wouldn't bother with makeup at all.

We can all be better than we think we are; enhancing what we have produces results. A five-minute makeup is a small investment that pays off in hours of good looks. Any investment you make in yourself will yield both dividends and interest—and in greater amounts than you anticipated.

CHAPTER TWO

The Ten-Minute Miracle

The Ten-Minute Makeup Inventory

The five-minute makeup inventory, plus:
Eye drops: the best eye freshener
Eyelash curler and *comb* or *brush*
Concealing cream
Lip pencils: colors that match your lipsticks, plus brown
Lip brush

Ten minutes may not sound like an awful lot of time, but it is doubling that of the basic makeup regime. The extra minutes are used in two ways. First, there is the perfecting of the application these minutes allow. Second are four touches that can greatly enhance your looks. You'll see that my ten minutes are indeed a great luxury.

I feel that our eyes are our greatest asset. They often speak for us and can make the difference between a pretty face and a truly stunning face. That is why I want to concentrate on them some more.

The use of eye drops, before applying any makeup, is very popular with European women and I hope that it will be equally in favor with American women soon. Eye drops clear the eyes of the natural day-to-day redness that detracts from their beauty, leaving them sparkling and refreshed. Strained, bloodshot, tired eyes won't be improved by makeup alone. Reliable brands work very well and don't require a prescription. All you need is a few extra seconds before starting your makeup, to allow the drops to work.

These seconds needn't be wasted, however. This is when you can use a rather old-fashioned gadget, but one that works surprisingly well—the eyelash curler. Correctly, intelligently used, it can help your lashes look longer and curlier. Most important is that the curler be used before any makeup at all is applied—which makes its use after the eye drops so convenient. Using it after the application of mascara or even foundation will cause that makeup to smudge and particles to get trapped in the little machine's parts.

The best results are achieved with a three-step plan. First use the curler at the very roots of the upper lashes. Press and hold for a minute. The curler should then be drawn farther along the length of the lashes to the middle and pressed in place for a half minute. You will get more of a curl this way than one pressing will give, and you will avoid an unnatural-looking abrupt upward jump of the lashes. The third pressing is done at the ends of the lashes, holding for another half minute.

After practicing you will know just how many pressings, and where, are best. Please remember never to use the curler after mascara has been used. It is not just a question of messing the mascara, but a far more serious matter of mascara sticking to the rubber strip on the curler, which in turn will cause your lashes to stick and be pulled out.

The next additional step comes *after* you have applied your foundation: the use of concealing cream, a marvelous item that helps you work some very special magic the rest of the world will know nothing about.

Concealing cream—or stick—has a wide variety of uses. It will help to cover darkness under your eyes, the natural darkness that

shows because the delicate skin in this area is transparent and re-
veals the tiny veins and tissues that lie under the skin. It also helps
hide blemishes or pimples that plague us.

Though many women use concealer under foundation, I prefer
the reverse. I think it's better to create a bit of coverage first with
foundation and then use the concealing cream to do any extra covering. The real mistake lies in choosing a product of the wrong
color, particularly a harsh white. White has a tendency to turn gray
on the skin and should never be used. At times even a shade that
looks dark in the jar will do a better job of covering than will a pale
shade. Never use too light a shade. To be most effective the concealer should match your foundation.

Careful application, as with any product, insures the best results.
Concealing cream should be dotted on with a fingertip, usually the
index or pinkie. Never rub it on, as that simply moves it around
without covering the area that most needs it. By dotting it on, you
will get the best coverage, right to the inner corner of your eyes,

where darkness is most often concentrated. When you do reach that inner corner, look upward and dot the cream all around until it is blended and smoothly covers the area.

It's always a good idea to blot lightly with a tissue to get rid of excess oils. If necessary, apply a second coat. Be sure to look at the area from all angles to be sure of an even, invisible film of coverage and protection.

Concealer should always be applied as finely and thinly as possible. If put on too thickly it will cake and crack during the course of the day or evening. Laughing, talking, smiling cause the makeup to fill in little lines on your face. Remember moderation. Dot, pat, blend thinly, and never rub.

After your rouge is in place and you're doing your eyes, you can pay extra attention to your mascara. If you didn't give your lashes a second coat before, now is the time to do it. Again, apply to the top of the lashes, sweeping outward to the tips, and then from underneath sweeping up. Don't forget your lower lashes. Recoating the lashes with a good, conditioning, lash-thickening mascara will help you have stronger, longer lashes.

As you recheck them in the mirror, make sure that the lashes are well separated. Using a lash comb or brush, pry between them just a little, being very careful not to hurt yourself and being very conscious of the delicacy and sensitivity of the eyes. The second coat of mascara should be applied as soon as the first is dry so that separating the lashes won't be too difficult.

To make eyes bigger and more sensuous, I suggest using your eyeliner underneath the bottom lashes. Again, apply it in dots, from the middle of the bottom lid to the outer corner, as this is where the lashes are naturally longer and fuller. As with the upper lashes, use your liner brush to make the dots, and then a cotton swab or fingertip to gently smudge them together. Your eyes will be open wide and your lashes rich. Once you get the knack of it, you'll realize what an easy trick this is.

I prefer dotting the liner instead of making one continuous line because my intention is to achieve as natural a look as possible. This is why I believe the best makeup is a subtle one, one that does the most with what you have rather than tries to correct.

Corrective makeup does not really correct. A product cannot change the shape of any of your features. It does make the flaws look noticeable. When I speak of contouring, and specifically of contouring the lips, I don't mean to try to change their shape at all. The contouring I am going to suggest is solely for the purpose of insuring a more perfect application of lipstick and of helping to eradicate what may be a problem for some women.

In the course of the day we talk, we smile, we kiss, we laugh, all with our mouths. We pout and our mouths become small; we grin and they widen. The mouth is an extremely mobile feature and we don't want to do anything to exaggerate it.

However, if you feel that you would like to give your mouth just a little more definition than can be achieved with only a lipstick, using a lip pencil will help. Select a pencil that most closely matches your lipstick and use it to outline your lips. Do not deviate from the natural line. Fill in the lips with your lipstick and you will have an impeccable mouth. The use of a defining pencil will eliminate the problem of lipstick running into those tiny lines above the upper lip.

For the woman who feels she has not been blessed with a full upper lip there is a good cosmetic trick that creates the impression of a fuller lip without looking obvious. First define both lips as I have indicated, using the color-coordinated lip pencil. Just within that line, on the center of the upper lip, draw a second one with the brown pencil. Fill in both lips with lipstick and watch the brown blend right in. It won't show as a separate color but will give the lip more body and a look of fullness. Add a bit of gloss, and that's all there is to it.

Using a lipstick brush takes a little longer than applying lipstick directly from the tube, but it is one of those tools that does impart a very professional, more finished look. The brush should put the lipstick only within your mouth's natural contours. It will not help restructure the geography of your face. Brushstrokes are very natural on the mouth, given the texture of the lips, but will look smeary and messy on the surrounding skin. One reason never to go outside your lips with lipstick is that the ingredients of this product were not made for facial skin, but only for the skin of the lips. Lipstick will sit on your skin; it won't blend in as it wears off your lips.

Makeup, whether you give it five or ten or five times ten minutes of attention, should always make sense. Don't try to mask or correct your features; it won't work. Good makeup was never intended to be a good camouflage. It can, however, show you at your strongest; it smooths and beautifies, enhances and ennobles . . . if you let it.

CHAPTER THREE

The Twenty-Minute Masterpiece

The Twenty-Minute Makeup Inventory

The five-minute makeup inventory,
The ten-minute makeup inventory, plus:
Exfoliating lotion
Foundation: liquid *and* cream
Highlighter
Optional: false eyelashes

Even the most formal makeup in the world is really nothing more than an extension of the basic makeup technique that you have already mastered. More time means that you will be free to perfect as well as add more variation and finishing touches to your total look.

Most women will feel that a special occasion, particularly an evening out or a formal daytime affair, calls for extra attention to their faces and will allow the extra time to permit the most exquisite, elegant makeup. It is wise to remember that "special" does not necessitate overdone; the good rules of makeup apply twenty-four hours a day. An elaborate event, one requiring formal fashion, does not mean an elaboration of your makeup to the point of exaggeration. That would always be wrong.

Twenty minutes means double and triple checking. It means being able to take your time. You won't be rushed and therefore you will be less liable to make mistakes.

You will, as always, start with a fresh, clean face. But now is the time to take your cleansing routine one step further by using an exfoliating lotion before your moisturizer.

The exfoliating lotion is a liquid product that freshens the face; it renews the surface of the skin by causing it to slough off the dead skin cells and unclog the pores. Saturate a cotton ball and stroke gently all over your face, using an upward motion. The result is a smoother, freer skin that is tightened and allows for a marvelous clarity in the makeup you will be applying. Follow with your moisturizer.

A second additional touch to consider is the use of two foundations, a liquid and a cream. For special evening occasions, use two.

Start with your regular daytime foundation and add to it. Using the same color, but in a cream form, reapply the foundation, particularly in the center of the face, the area that attracts more attention

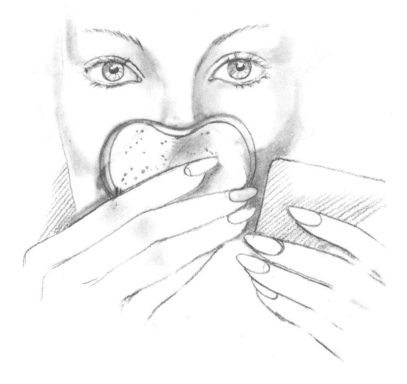

and receives more light. Apply both with a sponge, rinsing it out after the first application so that it's clean for the second. Blend the second very carefully over the first. What you are achieving is a polished, almost flawless finish.

It is a good idea to blot the face with a tissue in between applications to remove excess oil; this will help set the stage for the next application.

It is important to use each foundation sparingly to avoid caking. Total blending of the two foundations is a must if you are to insure no demarcation line. Remember that the point is not to show how many products you are using or how cleverly but to give yourself the best possible look with no visible effort.

A very beautiful finishing touch is highlighting, which is what the cosmetic industry calls the lovely light product. It is a light, frothy, whipped-creamlike fluff that is patted on at the end of your makeup when everything else is in place. When your nose is powdered to perfection, when your lips are deliciously shiny and your eyes are devastatingly done, that is when you add this subtle glitter. Pat it only at the very top of your cheekbones, quite close to the outer corners of your eyes, and then only a touch.

Highlighting cream is one product that should be applied only with your fingertips. A sponge would dull it. Squeeze a drop on your index finger and rub it with your other index finger to assure an even amount on each. Pat it on, one cheek at a time. Blend it in well, making sure you leave no fingerprints; that can happen easily. The shiny finish is due to mother-of-pearl compounded in the product. How exotic!

Used sparingly at the top of your forehead, highlighting cream leaves a beautiful glow. A tiny touch of its sheen at your temples or just above the brows is lovely too. But don't use too much or the effect will resemble perspiration! Remember that practice combined with careful application can take a little makeup a long way, and that less is always more elegant than too much.

This reminds me of another good thing that is often overused: false eyelashes. With today's mascara formulations, all of which are so improved, false eyelashes are no longer as popular as they were just a few years ago. Mascara alone can give you thicker lashes in an instant without the effort it takes to properly apply false ones. But in some instances false eyelashes are needed; sometimes mascara can

do only so much. When they are used they must be put on flawlessly.

The most important point about false eyelashes (which I examine thoroughly in "A Look at the Eyes") is the selection of the lashes themselves. There are many on the market that are very good. I prefer to think of them as extra lashes, ones that will add to the fullness of your own. No matter what your coloring, dark-brown lashes are the best—black ones are too thick and hard-looking. With the use of mascara the tips of the brown lashes will darken in a most natural way.

Putting on your extra lashes for the first time or the first few times should not be part of your first twenty-minute routine, or even your second. You will need time to master their usage. When you're putting on a special makeup for a formal occasion, don't attempt to experiment with lashes; it is simply not the right time. But when you have the extra-lash routine down pat, applying them can be fitted into your twenty minutes, and quite comfortably.

There will always be important events for which you will want to look your best and for which you will be prepared to take all the time necessary. But remember that makeup that becomes too overly important is more likely than not to turn out to be overdone. Remember that you should always want to look your best and not look like someone different for each occasion.

CHAPTER FOUR

The Three Faces of You

Although a woman is as complex as a precious jewel, in today's hectic world few have the time, money or the inclination to embellish every facet. I know many ladies, but very few who have ladies' maids. There are no more women like the empresses of old who could spend their days lavishing all their attention on their bodies and their wardrobes.

Today most women lead three different lives and are called on to change from one to the other to the third like chameleons. You must change your look to adapt to the indoor working activities of the weekday, the outdoor leisure life of the weekend, and the night life with its formal, social aspect.

As different as these three spheres are, so are the moods, the clothes and the makeup that are appropriate for each—all of which I want to explore with you to help you look and feel your best always.

Daytime: Outdoors

Americans are an outdoors-loving people. Perhaps it is because of the enormous size and diversity of the country that we seek so many outdoor sports and activities. Perhaps it is because Americans have more time for leisure than the peoples of other countries. In fact, American designers were the ones to invent what we call sportswear, the comfortable separates that are the mainstay of most women's wardrobes—the shirts, the sweaters and the jeans that are identified with the American look.

You will want a casual look in makeup to go along with this very casual dress. But before we can get to makeup itself we must consider light, the natural daylight you will be seen in. It is the strongest power in the world; artificial light can't even come close. Anything seen in natural light will be seen in the utmost clarity; it allows nothing to be concealed. Being a natural element, it does not look kindly on anything artificial. What you put on your face for a day spent out of doors will have to stand up to the closest scrutiny.

Because of the nature of outdoor activities you need the simplest, freshest look possible. Though this is the lightest of your three looks, it is still very important from both the beauty and skin-care points of view. Fresh air may be very good for you, but these days no one is quite sure how much of our air is really fresh. Pollution ravages complexions and landscapes alike. The dirt and irritants in the air are terrible for the skin, as well as for the eyes, the lungs and every other part of the body they reach. Your makeup is a very protective screen, the only one between you and pollution.

The sun can also be devastating. Too much sun can dry out the skin, causing a condition that outlasts the tan it gives. Whether you are lying in the sun, playing tennis on a court or watching from the stands, you have to be careful and protected from overexposure, which doctors now link to skin cancers.

Wind can be a negative beauty factor also. It may feel wonderful blowing through your hair, but windburn can be as damaging to the skin, and lips especially, as is sunburn.

There are a myriad of products available for controlling the degree of sun you want to get. They range from items that encourage the skin to tan—blocking out the burning rays—to those that block out all rays entirely. Athletes frequently use sun-block on their shoulders and arms, all exposed areas of their skin. The best cosmetically formulated ones are moisturizing as well. But for your face there is really nothing more effective than a complete, careful makeup application. With moisturizer as a base, foundation, rouge, eye shadow and lipstick all combine to form beautiful layers between your complexion and the elements.

Of course you don't want to go to the beach made up for a formal party, but that isn't what daytime makeup is really about. The casual look pretends that you have little or, better yet, no makeup on and is achieved with the deft use of your cosmetics. The trick and beauty of it is that none really shows.

This is my aim in using all makeup. Not only should you never look made up; for daylight activities you should also look especially understated and natural. Care is the most important factor here. As always, constantly blend—rouge into foundation, eye shadow into foundation—to make sure there are no telltale demarcation lines; that is the first priority.

Eye shadow should be limited to the area from the roots of your lashes to the crease on the upper lid. If you are very active outdoors, choose a lighter shadow—a pastel or neutral shadow—than you would normally use. Add a touch of color under the bottom lashes for that pretty continuation of color from the upper inner corner to a midpoint under the lower lashes.

If you are planning to wear false lashes, they should be scrupulously clean. Any old makeup or glue adhering to them is sure to show in daylight. Unless your activity is a wedding or garden party, they are really not needed. Mascara, always in good quantity, will give you a much more appropriate effect.

Double-checking your makeup is a must now. Although a well-lighted makeup mirror is also a must for daytime makeup, I suggest another check—by the natural light itself. Go to a window with your hand mirror and examine your face carefully. The natural light will show mistakes in color and application that the best indoor lighting will miss.

Daytime: Indoors

If you are making up for the day, but for inside an office, for example, the makeup approach is different. The lighting in an office or store or building is closer to the artificial light of your home than it is to daylight. Artificial light has a draining effect on colors as opposed to daylight, which accentuates them.

Long strips of fluorescent lighting can have a ghastly effect on everyone. If your company will permit it, it is worth the expense to change to softer pink bulbs, which will give much better lighting. If that isn't possible, I suggest buying a small desk lamp and using a pink bulb in it. This will give you at least a more flattering light and will be better for your eyes if you do close work.

Makeup that must take you through the business day needs careful attention too. To keep it long-lasting, go very lightly on moisturizer and foundation. Both are absolute musts, but both are also creamy substances that tend to melt under the stresses of heat and light. Apply them very sparingly, using only what you need for perfect coverage, tissuing off any excess before going on to the next step. Check your makeup in a mirror at home in a light closest to the one at work. If your face loses its glow at the office, correct it with a brighter shade of rouge, not a brighter foundation.

If you work in an office, whether as a receptionist, a secretary or an executive, your eye makeup has to be given new consideration. Dealing with people in these conditions puts you on an entirely different plane from that of normal social situations.

When with people socially, you communicate on the same height level, whether you are seated or standing. But when you are at your desk, you are frequently greeting people who are standing while you are seated; you look up at them. If you are doing paperwork during your discussion with them, you are frequently looking down. As you look in these different directions, very often several times in the course of one conversation, you expose different parts of your eye area. Lowering the lid, raising the brow, exposing the upper part of your lashes that remain visible when your eyes are open and you're looking straight ahead—all these positions call for very careful grooming.

Be aware of how your eyes look from all angles. Your eye shadow has to be well applied and fully blended so that shadow on your lids doesn't stick out like stripes of color when the lids are lowered.

Use a lash brush or comb to keep lashes separated.

If you use liner, make sure that it is evenly smudged to a flattering smoky effect and is not extending into the outer corner of your eye as an unnatural little curve.

The grooming of the brows is important too. Make sure you have a natural-looking brow, not a straight line of color that will look like a streak of dirt to someone looking down at you.

Because the workday for most people is at least seven hours long, you should do everything to insure the staying power of your morning makeup, giving it only a light touch-up at lunchtime. Pressed-powder shadows, rather than creams, provide long-lasting color. Mascara will last longer if lashes are treated to a light coating of face powder before its application.

Foundation and rouge can be given a longer life if you use my ice-cube trick after all your makeup is applied, *unless* you use face powder—patting the ice cube over that will cause makeup to cake. However, patting the face gently with your hands after rinsing them in very cold water and drying them will work well with the powder and feel great.

Nothing will keep you from biting, chewing and simply talking your lipstick off. It must be reapplied for a fresh, bright smile.

There are products available, similar to skin toners and lotions, that can be applied over makeup to set it in the morning. Pat one of these on with a cotton ball and use it at midday to freshen your face instantly. A small bottle of this liquid should be part of your desk-drawer kit.

Whether you keep this kit of makeup in your desk drawer or in your purse, it should contain everything you need for a touch-up or a fresh application if you are planning to go out for the evening after work. The kit should be a mini-collection of the products you use at home, with everything in small containers in the simplest possible form. Lipsticks and eye shadows have built-in applicators. Cream rouge can be put on with the fingers if you don't want to carry a sponge with you. However, it is a good idea to have at least one sponge for a new application of moisturizer, foundation and rouge, as it can be easily rinsed out after each use. Makeup-remover pads are a terrific convenience for getting a new start in the office washroom or at your desk. Mascara in this special instance can be re-applied rather than removed first, but lashes won't be easily separable. Check the inner corners of the eyes, as this is where color and dirt collect. Use a cotton swab to gently remove any accumulation before starting your new makeup.

Your kit should also hold a couple of pencils for quick eye-shadow touch-ups; emery boards for nail mishaps; a purse-size perfume atomizer or spray cologne; a comb and/or brush with a styling handle for perking up your hairdo. If you have the time, the place and the privacy for an instant hairsetter, by all means use it.

For the evening, whether you are doing a new makeup at home or merely freshening up at the office, it is not necessary to use a totally new palette of colors or a different range of products. I feel that livable, believable evening makeup is achieved with two variations on the daytime procedure: the quantity of makeup used and the dramatization of the eyes.

The quantity of makeup is very important because of the draining effect of artificial lights, which is even more acute in the evening. More eye shadow and more mascara make you look more exciting and luscious at night.

More rouge certainly. But, again, not necessarily in a different color. Rouge is not a fashion element but something that becomes a part of the complexion itself, like foundation. Your daytime foundation is the right nighttime foundation too, always as close to your natural skin tone as possible. Choose a brighter lipstick shade than your daytime favorite—this color change is a good one. Lipstick is one makeup element that must take its cue from your clothes, so be careful about the shade and follow the suggestions in "A Word on the Lips."

Face powder should always be used sparingly, but especially so at night, when it tends to obscure the light and bright effects of the other products. The most important place for it is on the nose, to prevent it from taking on a shine. Your chin might need it too if it tends to be oily.

And don't forget highlighter!

A perfectly good makeup, as outlined above, can be accomplished in the ladies' room at your job or wherever you have access to a mirror and running water. But if you are having a big night out and you have the time to prepare for it, you should treat yourself to that

extra care. I like the idea of perfecting more than one aspect of yourself, so that you can show more of those different facets I spoke of before. If you've spent all day looking businesslike, then the evening is the time to put all of that behind you as you go forth to dazzle. With the same basic components you can look as different at night as the career woman looks from the sporty, active woman. I don't suggest radical changes that would mystify those around you, but you may surely look as different as the fashions you wear for each activity.

If you are dressing at home for the evening, by all means take the time to start your routine with a beauty mask. Provide yourself with a beauty salon feeling. Put on the mask, stretch out with your feet up, and rest and relax for a half hour. Enjoy the refreshing feeling of pads over your eyes as the mask works its magic. When you rise you'll feel as though you've just come back from a marvelous vacation. This is the best beginning you can give to any evening.

A woman can be a fabulous creature at night. The fantasy permitted by the fashions for evening wear can release the creative spirit in every woman and send it soaring. Your look can be whatever pleases you the most, from a bird of paradise to an angel of the evening. You can shine, you can sparkle, you can explode with colors and textures, jewels and embroideries, furs or feathers. In my dictum of appropriateness I include an important concept, that of proportion.

If your evening fashion is indeed a fantasy of color, a brilliant brocade, a dazzling embroidery or, perhaps, smashing sequins, your face should not be in competition. Such styles call for an understated face, one whose cool composure will not fight with the brilliance of your dress but will rather offset it. Going a shade lighter in the selection of your foundation could be excellent in such a case. Pale, clear, understated—that is the best approach to important gowns or jewels, the refined look of utter elegance.

On the other hand, if your clothing is understated—its main feature being its superb silhouette or its magnificent draping or its singular color and texture—your face should provide the counterpoint, with all the fine drama you can carry. Brilliant eyes, shiny lips and cheeks, a glowing aliveness that can be a little more daring because of the simplicity of the fashion you have selected.

Makeup and fashion should always complement each other. A

sense of proportion is necessary for unity in your look; there is no place for a battle for attention here.

I think that the basis of looking right in any situation is the sense of being in tune with time and place. The occasion, the setting, your clothes and your makeup mood must all be of the same cast. It's as obvious as not wearing an evening gown to the office or sneakers to a wedding (well, *most* weddings). You wouldn't make such an obvious fashion mistake; now you must learn not to make the same kind of mistakes with your makeup. Don't groom yourself for a day of hiking as you would for a night at the theater. There are many, many aspects of yourself that are beautiful but would be wasted if shown at the wrong time.

Application, appropriateness, attitude—the three essentials to the three faces of you. Your intelligence in discerning and using them is what will make an ordinary woman extraordinary. Impeccable *application* of makeup + *appropriateness* to the occasion = *knowing* you look good—the only attitude that can make it all true! That is the easy equation you are going to master.

Part II

THE HEALTHY FACE

CHAPTER FIVE

Skin Care

Before discussing the makeup itself we should consider the canvas on which it is to be applied: the face, and hopefully, the healthy face. We must remember that the skin of the face as well as of the entire body is a very special living organ. It requires the greatest care to keep it in good working condition. It has to be protected from hot and cold, both of which can dry it terribly. Every inch of skin—on our legs, our arms, everywhere—needs conditioning with a good lubricant.

Everyone is born with beautiful skin. We always hear about the perfect skin, a baby's skin, and constantly strive to make our skin baby-soft once again. Ideal skin has a velvety surface, even tone, close, refined pores, a firm texture. As we grow up the pores enlarge, they clog. We develop blackheads, pimples and blemishes. Too much exposure to the elements and a lack of care damage the skin. We must start defending it.

Makeup itself, if not properly removed, can clog pores and mar the complexion. Even the finest foundation is meant only to beautify during the day or evening. Complete makeup removal is essential. You must cleanse your face at night, as even beautiful makeup can hurt your skin.

Cleansing your skin at night will help nurture it while you sleep. Cleansing it in the morning will give you a more beautiful look: clean skin reacts best to makeup.

Cleansing does involve more than soap and water. And cleansing the skin is not enough. Cleansing products contain ingredients that are not designed to stay on your skin. They are put on, they serve their very good purpose, and they should leave. Actually, the cleanser must be removed, and the ideal medium for the job is a skin lotion. Just as you would need water to remove soap (though you don't need or want either), you need a lotion to rinse off those last remaining traces of cleanser, and occasionally makeup. The lotion, or toner, is a clear liquid with which you saturate a cotton ball to apply to your face. It freshens, refines pores and perks up your skin wonderfully. There are lotions for all kinds of skin, such as, for example, astringents for oily complexions.

Just as you shouldn't cleanse without toning, you shouldn't cleanse and tone without nourishing your skin. You understand the importance of feeding your plants and flowers with water and polishing your wood furniture with oils; it is just as important to lubricate your skin, so that its beauty will be longer-lasting. Wrinkles and lines will appear eventually, but lubrication can postpone their appearance.

If you are cleansing and toning before a makeup, you will lubricate with a moisturizer. If you are cleansing and toning before retiring, you will use a more nourishing lubricant that will feed the skin as you sleep. Remember that a moisturizer can't reach the pores through makeup; it must be put on before. A night cream or lubricant may feel soft over a dirty face, but it won't be performing fully. The three steps are very closely linked: cleanse, tone, nourish. And this same system benefits each skin type.

There are really only three skin types: oily, dry and combination. The way to classify your type is to determine the quality of the greater portion of your skin. If your skin is very shiny, if you can feel the oil when you touch your face, yours is oily. If your skin chaps easily in cold weather and tends to be flaky, it is dry.

I do not consider "normal" to be a real skin type. Few women have a perfect, flawless complexion—everyone has trouble spots. A shiny nose and forehead with dry cheeks, for instance, is a combination complexion. For some women the type may not be as easy to define. Your skin may feel all right, but examine it closely. It may be a little drier around the eyes than you may wish or a little oilier in the center of your face. This is a combination skin.

Oily Skin

Although oily skin is generally associated with younger women, and dry with older women, at times mature skin too may have a few oily areas. Oily skin is constantly shiny, it perspires easily, has open pores and a tendency to form blackheads and blemishes. In youth it is very acne-prone.

Oily skin does not hold makeup well or for very long. After makeup has been applied the color seems to disappear; it sinks into the skin and frequently changes color. Foundation may turn orange, a powder, yellow. Oily skin needs frequent attention, but it is certainly not cause for despair. You can correct oily skin with a little time and effort and quickly see noticeable signs of improvement.

The most effective cleanser for oily skin is a water-soluble milky liquid or a light, vanishing cold cream. I prefer the milky cleanser because it rinses off so ideally with water. Beauty grains or scrub creams are an excellent once-a-week treatment for young oily skin.

Daily, thorough cleansing of an oily face is a guarantee of improvement because it gradually discourages oil production beneath the surface of the skin. Washing your face every hour with soap and water is not the answer, because your skin will fight back against the sudden shock by secreting more oil. This is a mistake many young people make, and it is a mistake because there aren't enough ingredients in soap alone to dermatologically correct the problem.

A soap that I do recommend is a medicated bar, to be used twice daily, after the cleanser, to help pores reach a balance in oil secretion. Modern multipurpose soaps perform miraculously because they are so much improved from the old concept of a detergent-action soap. They start the fight, with the milky cleanser, against oil.

A skin freshener and toner should be used after you have rinsed off every trace of the cleansing agents, when your face is really clean. The proper one for oily skin is an astringent or a medicated lotion that tightens the pores and skin. The astringent is a key product for your skin type because it gets beneath the surface of the skin to cleanse pores thoroughly. It penetrates deeply to the oil glands to help correct the oil secretion while it tones and freshens at the skin's surface. By stroking your face with a cotton ball that has been saturated with the liquid, you wipe away deep-down dirt and oil and leave your skin as clean as it can be.

The ingredients in these products, while getting rid of dirt and excess oil, do take away too much of the oils that are essential. Along with the oil the skin loses some of its moisture, which must be replaced. The ideal lubricant here is a lightweight, whipped moisturizing lotion or cream, which should be used very sparingly before makeup and a touch more generously at night. It will replace the moisture lost through cleansing and restore the skin to its proper pH balance—the equal acid and alkali concentration of the skin—without adding any oil.

At times even an oily skin may need extra lubrication for certain areas. If you are in your thirties, an eye cream is in order, no matter how oily your skin is. You should make sure that this delicate area gets the proper amount of pampering. There are no oil glands under the skin of the eye area, and it therefore needs all the help we can give it. A throat cream is advisable if the skin of your throat is dry. The cream will prevent early aging and that crepe-y Somerset Maugham skin.

Masks are wonderful ideas because they too help correct the skin's secretion of oil, making skin look and feel better. A beauty mask is an immediate conditioning of the skin; it's like spending a day at a spa. The best ones contain special tightening ingredients, absorbing clays and an astringent—all the elements needed to make your skin cooler and fresher. There are several different types of masks for oily skin, all of which work well: the peel-off mask; the cream mask; the powdered mask you mix yourself. I prefer the cream mask with its medicated base and pleasant fragrance. These are used like packs and are left on for five or ten minutes and then rinsed off. Astringent masks go deeply into the pores, tightening and refining them, and are left on for ten to thirty minutes. When using masks, always

avoid the eye area which has no reserves and should be treated to an eye cream while the mask dries.

When shopping for both the proper skin-care and makeup products for your skin type, look at the labels, which should specify that the product is for oily skin, problem skin or normal-to-oily skin. Because manufacturers make sure that packaging labels and instructions are clear, you can trust them and follow the label and instruction sheet enclosed in all packages. That is the best way to get maximum performance from the items you buy.

MAKEUP

When you buy your makeup for oily skin, there are three labels you should look for. Those marked water-based, oil-free, or minimum-oil content are all right for you.

Dry Skin

This skin looks transparent and flaky in certain areas around the nose, on the bridge of the nose between the brows, and around the lips. It may crack easily in winter months and gets burned quickly if exposed to the sun or wind. Because it is so thin and transparent, underlying veins are often noticeable.

Dry skin forms extra easily around the already oil-poor eye area.

Dry skin needs a lot of lubrication and has to be cared for like a baby. "Lubrication" is the key word. Even a cleansing cream can be beneficial if you use one that is specially formulated for dry skin. Using soap on dry skin is the ultimate sin (unless you are using one of those terrific superfatted, see-through lubricating soaps); regular soap will chap skin faster than harsh weather will.

The products you buy should be labeled as good for normal-to-dry skin, dry skin or sensitive skin. Your cleansing cream should be a melting type, of a petroleum jelly consistency. As it touches the skin it melts every bit of grime and makeup, which can then be tissued away. Dirt leaves the pores and comes to the surface, to be removed with the cream. A soft, clean facecloth or cotton pads can be used instead of tissues, if you prefer.

The second step in the three-part skin-care technique for dry skin is toning. Toning lotion must be alcohol-free; to be preferred are those with herbal extracts, rose water, orange blossom water and perhaps witch hazel too—always nonalcoholic. Although toners may look alike—and are applied with cotton balls—never mistake an astringent—clear and innocuous as it may appear—for a toner. There is quite a difference between a dry-skin toner and an astringent, and that difference will determine whether or not you'll get the results you want.

Lubrication follows toning. In the morning, lubrication takes the form of a moisturizer applied perhaps with a sponge. It should always be of a consistent formulation—not just a light, thin, filmy type. It should be labeled a moisturizing complex for dry skin, containing more than one lubricant, to assure total penetration and complete daytime protection. Never apply makeup to the skin directly. Dry skin will flake without moisturizer as a base, and you may end up with blotchy patches, as the foundation or rouge may "take" more to these flaky areas around the nose, forehead and mouth. Moisturizer equalizes the skin's texture and assures a very smooth application of makeup and a longer-lasting one too.

For nighttime you have two, three or more creams to use in rotation. Rotating is vital because dry skin gets used to a cream very easily and stops its performing action. The skin builds up a resistance just as the body does when given the same kind of medicine over a period of time. The skin needs variety. This involves a slightly greater investment at the beginning, but it does pay in the long run since you are not using more cream. Rather, you are using each cream at a slower rate. (During hot summer months, store the creams in the refrigerator to preserve them.)

Rotate your creams constantly, and if possible, don't use any one more than two or three times a week. Ideally, you should have a lubricant with hormones, another with protein, another with vitamins. Your skin will be very grateful for this varied diet and you will notice results.

The creams should be applied with your fingertips in the smallest amounts; even though your skin is dry, it cannot absorb large quantities of cream at once. If you go to sleep with too much on, the excess will be absorbed into your pillowcase. A dab will vanish into your skin and only you will know it's there. Remember that a regular routine of a little is more beneficial than bursts of too much.

Being gentle at all times is very important for dry skin because it can be stretched and damaged so easily. Learn to give yourself a lubricating, moisturizing mini-facial at home, using little movement of your fingertips. Pat around the eyes, stroke lightly on your cheeks and forehead and nose, pat the neck upward. All these movements stimulate your circulation, which in turn helps the skin absorb the cream faster. You have to work the cream into the skin; it won't penetrate by itself.

Dry skin also needs the help of eye cream, throat cream and beauty masks. Eye cream is needed because of the absence of oil glands in that area. Throat cream is needed to tighten that area and delay wrinkling and sagging. Though both should be used at night, a light film of eye cream can be used during the day under makeup.

A deep-penetrating performing cream, which is applied only once or twice a month, produces excellent results.

Dry-skin beauty masks act as mini-facials that firm the skin. Rather than using such a mask once or twice a week, I suggest using it every day for one solid week out of every month. The results are phenomenal. All masks are good. The best are those based with seaweed; those based with hormones; those based with fruits and essential oils. While creams take time to show results, masks work immediately. I love them.

A double-action mask treatment that is great for the skin consists of an invisible film of nourishing cream *plus* the mask, applied over it. As the mask solidifies, the cream is virtually pushed into the skin, penetrating faster than it would as a regular application. And you get double the benefit.

MAKEUP

The ideal foundation is a creamy liquid or creamy compact, particularly those packaged with their own sponges. If your skin is very dry, use a foundation with an oil separation, shaking the bottle thoroughly to mix the color sediment with the added oil.

Although many people think that face powder is drying, I do not. Modern powders are very thin and not at all harmful to delicate skin. A light veil of powder on the nose—even the driest one—will give the makeup a finished look.

Combination Skin

This skin type is the most prevalent. It is most often characterized by dry skin around the eyes or a very rich oily center of the face or both. This skin needs a little more attention and care, but the results will be terrific.

The skin care for combination skin is a sum of the best of both the oily method and/or the dry method of cleansing, to suit your own special needs.

A careful overall cleansing with a mild, water soluble cleansing cream, a mild cleansing milk or a vanishing cold cream is the first step. A skin toner recommended for normal skin—one that is neither high in alcohol content nor completely alcohol free—is the delicate skin lotion you should use.

Now specific problem areas need special pampering. For oily areas take a few seconds to thoroughly scrub with an astringent; usually the nose or the entire "T" area is oil-prone. I always advise a

generous amount of daytime moisturizer on drier areas—often the cheeks—and only the lightest touch on overly oily areas.

Night lubrication with eye and throat creams is in order, but for those special dry places only.

Beauty masks are particularly beneficial. A slightly drying mask for normal-to-oily skin, with a light veil of lubricating cream used under it on dry areas, is one possibility. A more nourishing mask for dry-to-normal skin can be used, but avoid oily areas when you apply it. For the best results, alternate between the two. If your dry areas are most prevalent, use only the mask for dry skin. If skin is most oily, use the mask for oily skin. Remember that the most prevalent condition requires the most attention and that all areas require some.

MAKEUP

Don't forget your moisturizer. Sponge application is wonderful here because you can reapply quickly on areas that need extra lubrication and you can wipe moisturizer off those spots that need less. A sponge does a neat, effective job where fingers and tissues become too clumsy. A sponge is never wasteful and is perfect for all skins.

Foundation should be for normal-to-oily skin as this will last the longest. By using extra moisturizer on drier areas, you will balance the effect of the foundation. A light use of powder on extra oily areas will increase the staying power of your foundation.

Skin Allergies

More and more people today seem to be plagued by allergy problems. I have found that it is usually not an allergy that has surfaced but rather a sensitivity to pollution, a reaction to the general stress of life, or a protest against the synthetics that surround us more and more and the lack of fresh air and good nutrition.

There is so little naturalness left in foods, especially those that are canned or frozen, because of preservatives and other additives. All these chemicals we are ingesting can eventually throw us off balance, and, falsely, we attribute a skin disorder to the last cosmetic we have bought, to a new color that has just been recommended, to a preparation we have been using.

Actually, the simplest internal medicine that may be prescribed can throw us off and cause reactions associated with an allergy—hives, for example. Try to recognize the difference between such an effect and an allergic reaction to a cosmetic before you throw out your new lipstick.

Often we do break out because of a certain product—not a new one but one we've been using for a long time. Again, this is the body's way of telling you it's had enough. Now is the time to try a different and new product.

Of course there are authentic cases of people who are allergic to strawberries or dust or pollen. Some cosmetics can certainly engender an allergic reaction—but these are cosmetics that I don't recommend under any conditions. Most specifically I'm talking about frosted beauty preparations—not the new colors and shades that have just a touch of shimmer but the garish frosteds made with synthetic or actual fish scales. The skin often rejects this ingredient and develops a blemish. Eye makeup allergies are often directly associated with the use of frosted shadows. The eyelid swells and the outlying area breaks out in a rash. Frosted nail polish can cause the same kind of eye irritation if you rub your eyes unconsciously.

The aroma of a new cologne can irritate your sinuses and your eyes. Testing new fragrances before you buy any can help you avoid an allergen. Before deciding that you are allergic to any one item, eliminate all other possibilities. And remember that only a doctor can confirm your suspicions. Finding makeup for sensitive skin is no longer a problem. Almost every major manufacturer has a full line of allergy-free products, giving you as much of a choice as you could want.

If you have an allergy, take heart. You have a wide spectrum of options to select from and are no longer limited in any way. With the right picking and choosing you will look beautiful and feel beautiful as well.

CHAPTER SIX

Nutrition and Exercise

Just as exercise and diet can benefit your body, proper nutrition and facial exercises can improve your face.

What you eat is very important: the well-being of your digestive system, and your entire body, shows readily on your face. Just as drinking too much can make us look and feel tired, malnutrition can be detrimental to your good looks. Chances are you aren't undernourished, but that doesn't mean you are getting the right nourishment.

Natural foods are always good. Fruit freshly picked is the greatest, purest food available—no preservatives, no additives, no artificial sweeteners. Fruit, citrus fruit especially, provides us with vitamin C, an important vitamin for good health. Vegetables, eaten raw or steamed, are another boon to our system. A carrot supplies all the vitamin A you need for a day and helps a lot more than your eyes. Vitamin A is vital for healthy skin and shiny hair. Nothing is more satisfying than a plentiful green salad dressed with vinegar and olive oil—fresh tomatoes, cucumbers and herbs, natural and delicious.

Whole grain cereals and wheat germ offer another health-giving vitamin—B. Yogurt is an all-purpose food that tastes good and is good for you. If you have allergies, yogurt can be of special help in minimizing the effects. It is a naturally fermented food that fights off germs in our system.

I am not a dietician, but the nutritional concepts I live by and suggest to you come from my great friend and a great nutritionist, Gaylord Hauser. All of the emphasis he puts on the use of natural foods I know to be beneficial to the skin as well as to the over-all health of the body.

Along with fresh fruits and fresh vegetables—oranges, peaches, apples, broccoli, spinach and string beans are all delicious examples—lean meats, chicken and fish are excellent protein choices. This natural way of eating isn't a reducing diet *per se*—although eating small quantities will always help you lose weight—but a lifelong diet for good health and a healthy, well-fed complexion. I think it's marvelous that nature has coordinated the proper diet for our inner selves as well as for our outer beings.

And just as I mentioned briefly before, the face can benefit from *exercise* as much as the body can. I personally love the expression lines that life and experience etch on our faces. It distresses me no end to see women so wrapped up in their vanity that they do not allow themselves the ordinary gestures and expressions of everyday living because they are so afraid of causing wrinkles. I think this is nonsense. I have sat across from women, trying to have an intelligent conversation, with someone who turns her entire body from side to side rather than use her neck to move her face, for fear of throat wrinkles. There are women who will not smile because they are afraid of causing lines to form around the mouth. If you are a sensible person, you'll think I'm inventing these cases, but I can assure you I'm not.

I do not consider a wrinkle a tragedy, although I know there are many who do. But rather than try to prevent the face from aging by ridiculously restricting those expressions that really are what our lives are all about, I prefer to include in our discussion of face care a series of simple facial exercises that will both help revitalize face muscles and retard the lining and sagging processes. I love these exercises, because not only do they help keep a face more vital and alive-looking but they are also great stimulants to the circulation. As

I've mentioned, anything that keeps the bloodstream in vigorous motion is greatly beneficial to the skin. Thus both the texture and the shape of the face will spark to these stimulations.

These exercises are based on principles of yoga that have been successful for many centuries. Just think of the serenely beautiful faces, clear and unlined, of so many women, and, yes, men too, from India, and you can see the sort of results I'm talking about. But don't look for miracles overnight. The principles, while being very sound, are not as fast-working as one might wish them to be. Although I have heard many claims of almost instantly induced well-being from people undergoing total yoga exercise programs, most benefits come during a long, faithfully executed regimen. Note that I said "during." Although the ultimate goal is a long-term achievement, there is always some definite improvement along the way. If it doesn't come overnight, neither does it come all at once, so you will have the satisfaction of seeing, and feeling, a definite enhancement before too long.

If you spend *ten minutes a day* going through the following routine, it should be enough. If you can and want to do more, marvelous. Do it. If there is one position that is directed toward a particular area you want to improve, spend more time on that one, doing it several times. At the end of each session your face should feel relaxed, the muscles well-stretched, the skin tingly with all the stimulation. Check the mirror and see how you look. Chances are you'll want to start exercising your entire body this way! But since it is your face that we are most concerned about here, let's concentrate on that.

What we start with is not really an exercise but an attitude.

RELAXATION
Before doing specific exercises it is most important to relax. This may sound like a waste of time, but when there is tension in the face, no exercise will be worth while. So lie flat on the floor and close your eyes. With your mind's eye, visualize your face. Now inhale and screw the face up into a tight tense *knot*. Use all the features. Experience the tightness and tension, and then, slowly exhaling with an audible sigh, completely relax your face. Feel all the tension float away, your face relaxed, the skin smooth. To make certain that you are not omitting any part of the face, start with

your scalp and forehead and literally suggest that each part of your head relax, then move to your eyes and eyelids, the nose, the cheeks, ears, lips, chin and neck. Just relax. If you put some cream on your face while you're relaxing you'll derive extra benefit.

BABY HEADSTAND

Good circulation is important for healthy skin, and the baby headstand is an easy way of improving circulation in the scalp, head and face. It also combats aging by reversing the pull of gravity.

Sit on your heels, knees on the floor, with your arms hanging loosely at your sides. Bring your head down to the floor in front of you and raise your buttocks up and off your heels. This will automatically change the position of your head, so do not move your head independently. To complete the pose (although if you can go only this far you are already deriving benefits), bring your heels up to your thighs and grasp hold of your ankles. Balance, and stay for a minute. Then release your ankles, bring your feet to the floor and sit back on your heels. Keep your head down for a few seconds, as coming up too quickly might make you feel dizzy.

EYE ROTATION

Since the eyes are the most looked-at part of the face, they should not be neglected. To keep the eye muscles strong and to rest the eyes and keep them bright-looking, the eye-rotation exercise is recommended.

Sitting comfortably, keep your head perfectly still and *move just your eyes*. Make clockwise circles, slowly going all around. Do this three times, trying not to miss passing any point around the outside of the eyes. Then go counterclockwise. Now close your eyes and rub your palms together vigorously; this friction creates warmth. Still keeping your eyes closed, cup your warmed hands over your eyes. Allow this velvety blackness that surrounds your closed eyes to soothe them. After holding for a few seconds, very slowly let your hands slide down your eyelids and cheeks until they rest in your lap. Now open your eyes and feel refreshed!

THE LION

This exercise restores good muscle tone to the neck and face and as a by-product is also excellent for the fingers, those important parts of the anatomy that are almost always exposed and rarely exercised.

Sitting on a chair or on the floor, inhale through your nose. (Always inhale through the nose; this filters the air.) Now exhale forcefully through your mouth and do the following three things:

a. Open the eyes wide and look up.

b. Open the mouth wide and stretch the tongue way out, as if you wanted to touch the chin with it.

c. Separate and stretch the fingers while pressing the heels of your hands on your knees.

Feel the pull, and then release the pose and relax. Mentally explore your face and see how it feels. The pull tells you which muscles are being used and stimulated.

THE BUBBLE

To help smooth out lines, blow up your mouth with air as if it were a balloon. Keeping the air trapped in your mouth, bring it all to the right cheek for a moment, then to the left, bring the air up under your nose and then down to your chin. Swiggle it around and then release it. Do this whenever you can during the day, when no one is watching, as well as during the exercise period.

THE GARGOYLE

This is helpful in preventing a double chin.

With your head down, pull your tongue back in your mouth and open your mouth as wide as you can. Keeping your tongue pulled back and your mouth still open, bring your head up and let it hang back. Clench your teeth. Do this a few times. You should feel this very powerfully in the neck area.

CHEWING

Good for the facial muscles, teeth and gums. Yogis say that you should chew liquids as if they were solid and chew solids until they're almost liquid. While this kind of chewing is not done publicly, you can easily do it when you're alone. This too is not really an exercise but a new habit to develop that will improve not only the facial muscles but your digestion, and thus your over-all well-being.

As with the skin care and maintenance programs we have talked about, these everyday activities take longer to read about and learn than to actually do! What sounds like a lot of work and a lot of effort is in reality translated into a few minutes of your day, each day. Once you become used to caring for your skin, it is as routine as brushing your teeth, and a lot more luxurious if you truly love the products you use and enjoy them as they're meant to be enjoyed, for their totally feminine texture and fragrance as well as for their glorious benefits. The minutes invested in daily skin care, choice of food, and exercise will add up to years of increased health and good looks for your whole lifetime.

If you live in a city where there are fine salons, or you can afford visits to the fabulous spas, of course you will want to utilize these professional facilities for meticulous skin care and grooming help. It's always marvelous to let someone else do the work for a change, and there are always new products and new tips to learn about. Most of the face-care routines I advocate and many of the products I use are the results of extensive experience with many women who come to the salons for help.

But even if pampered, expert care is not part of your budget or travel plans, the *results* can be easily duplicated at home by you with the investment of time and care that you give yourself. If you cannot afford the larger luxury that spas and salons provide, enjoy the small richness of self-indulgence that is yours alone to give . . . to you. No one in the world can really be as good to you as you can be to yourself. It is not charity but *loving-kindness* that should begin at home, beginning with yourself in the care you give yourself. It is also true that the more you care for yourself, the more others will care for you too, in the physical and every other sense. The time to start is *now*.

Part III

APPLICATIONS

CHAPTER SEVEN

At the Beginning

The most basic item for the majority of women is foundation. A more recent innovation than eye or lip color, it is the cosmetic that most women recognize as a necessity, yet a surprising number don't use it properly. They make mistakes when choosing the color and/or the consistency, and when applying it, frequently use too much. Many women don't realize that they don't need to use it at all—or maybe only a little.

Let's talk about foundation itself for a moment. Like so many of our preferences and ideas on beauty, foundation originated in Hollywood. Makeup men had to develop a skin covering that would hold up to studio lights as well as photograph attractively. At first, it was very much like the theatrical greasepaint used by stage actors throughout the world. Foundation was then exceedingly thick as well as greasy and gave much more coverage than was necessary. Soon actresses began to develop skin problems that damaged their valuable faces. New formulas evolved, and foundation changed from a stick to a cream.

It was then packaged in jars and was thinner and creamier than the old "paint," making it easier to apply. But even so, not everyone needed the coverage necessary for stage and film. The American woman wanted a new, thinner formula, and she got one. Cream foundation became the even lighter liquid that is most popular today.

Within that bottle there were soon further modifications: a light, water-based foundation that didn't need to be shaken, which provided enough coverage for young, smooth faces; a heavier oil-based type made for extra coverage.

The cosmetics industry went even further, developing over-the-counter products for every woman's needs. Foundations now come in cake compacts, bottled liquids, creams in jars and, most recent of all, the gel foundation in a tube for a sheer, see-through look. This truly formidable array of products to choose from can make it quite bewildering for a woman to find which is right for her special needs.

The first thing to consider is whether you need a foundation and what you want it to do. Foundation performs two separate functions—covering and coloring. The two are very different.

I believe that covering is very important. A covering foundation can blend the skin tones of your face to a smooth evenness. There are very few complexions of perfect, uniform tone (which is why most women use foundation). This is true of everything in nature: the natural look, whether of the skin of your face, the hair on your head or the leaf of a tree, is composed of a number of shadings of a color. Foundation acts as an equalizer, bringing differences in color together, but not so unified as to resemble a mask.

The imperfections that can be covered include what we call *couperose*, those tiny broken blood vessels that occur so frequently near the nostrils and tend to show up as a pinkish flare. Perhaps the nose itself is too rosy compared with the rest of your complexion and needs to be toned down. There may be dark shadows around the eye area, the result of uneven pigmentation or skin that is very thin and transparent.

A sudden blemish may appear. You may have acne scars to cover. Women who are on the pill may develop brown spots or a tarnishing of the skin which need covering. All of these problems can receive full benefits from the use of foundation. However, the coverage doesn't have to be applied all over your face. If you don't need total coverage, use foundation sparingly. If you are one of the lucky few with fine, clear skin, please consider not using foundation at all.

I don't believe that foundations should be used for changing the color of the complexion. Though many feel that foundation can make miraculous changes—such as going from pale to tan in the middle of winter—I don't agree. You cannot color your face to look suntanned without painting every other exposed part of your body, such as your hands and legs. And no matter how refined foundation is today, it cannot believably imitate the effects of the sun.

I love to see a face that has a believable finish to it. A foundation should be like your second skin, blending totally with your natural coloring. The one you select should be in a shade that resembles your own skin as closely as possible. Finding the right foundation tone for your face is very simple. Yet when I watch women in stores selecting this important cosmetic, I am shocked to see that they (as well as the cosmeticians, who certainly should know better) test the colors on themselves in a really meaningless way. By this I mean the practice of stroking a bit of color on the back of the hand.

Stop for a moment now and go to the nearest mirror—I want to show you something. Hold the back of your hand out against the side of your face, fingers pointing upward, so that the skin of the hand can be seen. Look at the colors of the hand and the face: they are completely different! Stroking foundation on the skin of your hand won't give you any idea of how it will look on your face.

What you do want is a shade to match your face, not your hand. The place to test for this is on the skin of the neck, just at the jaw. The foundation should blend in perfectly with the skin tones of this area so that when you apply it to your face there is no demarcation line. Perfect matching will also eliminate the need to bring the foundation all the way down to the base of the throat, not to mention the unnecessary dry-cleaning bills for stained necklines and collars.

The truly best test of all for foundation is trying it directly on your face. Even fully dressed in a department store, you can easily remove a bit of the foundation you have on. The salesperson at the counter can give you a tissue or a cotton ball for this purpose (every cosmetic counter has them). It is very important to take the little bit of time to do this. There is no substitute for the proper choice of foundation. I cannot stress the importance enough; even if you do everything else correctly, without the right foundation all your attention will be wasted.

I know as you read this, many of you who don't like your skin color are thinking that this is marvelous advice for the fortunate few. "What am I to do with my sallow [or ruddy or ashy or dull] complexion?" I can almost hear you. I want to say now that my solution involves the correct use of rouge, which creates a glow that counteracts these skin-color problems. Remember that you can't change the color of your skin without the effort showing. But you can effectively use makeup, and in this case rouge, to help soften and play down problem areas.

To me the face is like a blank canvas waiting for the artist to paint a picture. The type of foundation you use depends on the look you want. Just as the artist works with media ranging from watercolors to oil paints, you have a great variety of foundations to choose from for the background of the picture you want the world to see.

A word of reminder: all foundations, regardless of their composition, must be put on after moisturizer. Though we have discussed this before, it doesn't hurt to repeat it—that's how important moisturizer is. It is a shielding agent that protects the skin from pollution by the ingredients in the makeup you put on over it. Moisturizer, in varying degrees, is important for every skin and should never be forgotten. Now to return to foundation.

The thin, liquid, water-based foundation is akin to watercolors; it provides the minimum coverage and gives a light look and feeling. This is a very natural, fresh, spontaneous look. It reminds me of pictures by such an artist as John Marin, whose paintings of sailboats and seascapes give just this kind of feeling. There is less sense of formality and pose than is present in an oil painting. The artist selects his medium for the kind of effect he is trying to achieve, and so can you. Much of the choice depends not only on the subject but also on the mood to be conveyed.

Certainly you choose your makeup to suit an occasion and the time of day for which it would be most appropriate. Whatever your selection, I do not want you to feel dependent on the foundation. For instance, you don't have to wear a heavy oil-based foundation on a formal occasion; this is not a hard-and-fast rule. In fact, heavy foundations can create problems for many women of all ages. On mature skin a heavy foundation sinks into wrinkles and lines it is meant to hide—if anything, emphasizing them more. Its use can worsen problems we associate with younger skins—blemishes and acne. Girls with problem skins try to hide discolorations and bumps under heavy layers of makeup. Rather than hide them, the heavy foundation aggravates them by further clogging pores.

The kind of foundation that will help you enhance your looks without drawing attention to its use is a thin foundation, either in liquid or gel form. Whether you want all-over coverage, an evening of tone or a sheer look, the gel will give it to you. Though generally younger girls prefer gel, I think mature women too should take advantage of the fresh, outdoorsy look the gel gives its wearer. I would hate to see the kids having all the fun. Why not try a sheer, sheer foundation? You may love it.

As I have said, my favorite application tool is the sponge; I have used it on some of the most famous faces in the world. Small, round cosmetic sponges are inexpensive, but their advantages are priceless. With just a little practice, you'll find that you are more adept at putting on your makeup than you ever thought possible. Unlike even the most agile fingertips, the sponge won't leave any traces of having been on your face. It can blend in foundation (and rouge, as you will see) faster than any other tool—and remember that perfect blending is the secret to perfect, velvety-smooth makeup.

The sponge applies and removes, depending on your needs. You won't be able to put on too much, as fingertips are so liable to do. The sponge releases foundation to your face automatically; there's no rubbing to hurt your delicate skin.

Simply rinse it out after you've used it and it will be ready for its next job again and again. You will always have a "professional" applicator at hand for very little cost. When one wears out it is easily replaced. Vive la sponge!

Now that you have one firmly in your hand, just rinse it under cold water and wring it out until it is barely moist, for the smoothest application. Apply foundation directly to the sponge or dot it on your face as discussed in the "Five-Minute Makeup"—this is a matter of choice. Then pat the foundation on rather than using the sponge in long strokes. Pat lightly, covering cheeks, forehead, nose and chin. Blend all areas carefully to eliminate any fine lines of distinction. When you're only using foundation on certain areas, make sure that the outer edges blend into your skin evenly. Remember that patting works very well for this spot-blending.

Always start at the center of your face and work upward when you want total coverage. Work toward the temples, the hairline. Work up the jawline from the chin. Work up rather than down, as that tends to cause sagging.

Examine your face carefully to make sure that coverage is flawless and even. If you can hardly see that it's on—wonderful! I recommend your using a two-sided mirror, one side of which magnifies. The magnifying side should be used to examine your blending, and the regular side used to check your over-all look.

Now is the time in the makeup routine when many women think about using face powder. Some women use it alone, without foundation—but using a moisturizer before is a must. Moisturizer application should be very correct, as any excess will attract excess powder and cause it to cake. Powder used on very good skin should be the no-color kind that gives a matte finish without changing the natural tone of the skin. Then go on to rouge.

But if you are using foundation, use your powder after you put on your rouge, not before. This is why a full discussion of powder ends up the chapter on rouge, "A Pat on the Cheek." (Depending on the foundation you use—many contain tiny particles of powder that will give you the same matte look—you may find that you don't need it at all.)

Making foundation last seems to be its biggest problem. Often foundation applied at the start of the day seems to disappear almost completely within a matter of hours, actually reappearing on hands and clothing—anywhere but where it belongs. One reason for this is that oily skin tends to soak up makeup. Occasionally it disappears because of a habit of constantly touching the face. Perhaps this is done unconsciously, but nevertheless it removes traces of makeup each time.

One trick I use to solve this problem is a simple one. When all of your makeup is on, get an ice cube from your freezer and pat your face very gently with it. Pat, pat, pat everywhere. This will set your makeup for hours without making it look artificial. There is one situation, however, where the ice cube will not work and that is if you've used powder. The wetness of the ice cube will cause it to cake. The variation of this procedure involves using your fingertips.

Run your hands under very cold water, dry them, and while they're still icy cold, pat, pat, pat.

You can repeat this later in the day if you feel your makeup fading; you don't need the ice cube when you have your fingertips always ready. Without applying makeup all over again, your makeup will come alive. The cold-water treatment is a good stimulant for skin as well as a revival for your makeup. Running your hands under cold water, from a faucet at home or in a brook in the country, is also very good for your nerves. It is a terrific relaxer for highly charged people, as it releases excess energy as lightning rods release electricity. (Running cold water over your wrists will cool your entire body, especially in the hot summer months.)

Just as cold fingers work for your foundation, you should let your foundation work for you—whether it's for all-over cover or simply to even out a tan (for instance, to blend in the areas left by your great big sunglasses). Once its function is understood, foundation becomes one of the most helpful tools in your beauty kit and certainly one of the most versatile.

CHAPTER EIGHT

A Pat on the Cheek

I love rouge. Once the proper foundation has been applied, there is no other cosmetic that can do so much for a woman—and for the people looking at her. And now that I have said what it is I love, I must tell you what I hate: using rouge to correct the shape or size of the face. It doesn't work.

What rouge can do, and do beautifully, is change the color and cast of a complexion by coloring the cheeks with a bright, beautiful glow. Skin that is too pale or too ruddy or too olive in tone can benefit from the careful application of rouge in a color that complements that of your foundation.

Rouge puts a blush, or glow, on your face that rivals natural blushing without being dependent on the emotions that cause it. The charm of an innocent young girl blushing high up on her cheeks is what we want to re-create with rouge, and as believably as possible. I want you to feel wonderful about yourself—and certainly not embarrassed.

Rouge has a magic to it, and like all magic, it must be carefully handled. A little rouge is good, a good amount is better, but too much, as with anything, can be an absolute disaster. Heavily rouge-reddened cheeks have no relationship to the good use of makeup. But a great deal of rouge can be applied with great results.

Rouge is available in various formulations, all of which you can test yourself at the cosmetic counters of department stores and salons.

There are the gels, the most recently developed of all rouges. If you are very young or if you have impeccable skin, a gel can make you look ravishing and as if you had nothing artificial on. Gels are made with an alcohol base, meant for oily skin, as it leaves no grease on the face, and with a water base.

The alcohol-based gel tends to be drying because of the pigments it contains. These pigments can collect around the hair follicles of the fine peachlike fuzz found on your cheeks and extending to your temples. These tiny coagulations can become quite noticeable by the end of the day.

The water-based gel provides a smoother application, but it has a diminished staying power.

As sponges don't work well with gels, fingertip application is a must. However, both gels stain fingers and must be washed off the hands right after they've been applied. Because of the drawbacks mentioned, their popularity is diminishing.

A totally different formulation is the brush-on dry blusher. This is the modern format of an old idea; dry rouge was used as movie makeup years ago. Blushers are wonderful because they are no longer drying, are far less concentrated (so you don't get too much on the brush) and come in a great variety of shades.

The blusher, in its neat compact complete with brush, is a terrific convenience product. Many women use this kind of rouge and this one alone.

But my favorite format is the cream rouge. It provides a very beautiful and very believable color. It is easily applied, either with the fingertips or, as I prefer, with a sponge. It travels well in its small jar, be it in your purse or in a carrying case. Its staying power is unbeatable. If your skin tends to absorb your makeup readily, you'll have no trouble in reapplying cream rouge, which alone can revitalize your entire face. (A terrific effect is achieved by using both cream and brush-on-rouge; more about that later.)

Two important aspects of cheek coloring must be understood: placement and color.

Rouge belongs on the cheeks. Even with those great cheekbones of Katharine Hepburn (or even Audrey), it is still a difficult matter to locate the right place for application.

I don't put rouge in the middle of the face or near the jawline or too close to the nose. One blushes and rouges the tip of the cheek, on the highest part of the bone. Smile and then touch your cheekbone. Keep smiling as you start the application, as smiling brings into prominence that highest part of the cheeks where the heaviest application goes.

The smoothest results are achieved with the use of a sponge. Fold the sponge in half, making a corner, and apply the rouge with that area to help you concentrate color only where you want it. With the greatest amount of color on the cheekbone, lighten your sponge strokes as you blend the outer areas toward the temples.

At this point check the color in the mirror. Chances are you will feel that you have applied too much. But don't remove any color;

wait until you have finished your eye and lip makeup, when you can see your rouge in relation to the rest of your face. It is the absence of the other makeup that makes the rouge look so prominent.

Check to see that the rouge is thoroughly blended. After the cheeks have been rouged, the color should lessen in density as you work it toward the temples and ears. Don't be afraid to have rouge near your eyes; the color can come close to the area shaded by the bottom lashes, because this creates a great outdoorsy look. And when you smile, your cheeks naturally rise toward your eyes, expanding as the eyes contract. This is a happy place for rouge to be. Color drawn into the area will complement your eyeshadow and emphasize the whites of your eyes.

Don't apply rouge to your chin. The chin is very close to the neck, which is of a paler cast than your face. A rosy chin would jut out and look wrong. There is an area of your neck that I do like rouging—the tendons that reach up behind your ears. If your hair is short or worn up and away from your face, a slight blush there looks very pretty—just a slight, light touch of color.

Though I prefer cream rouge for most cheek coloring, it is great to combine it with the brush-on powder blusher, since they work very well together. As the cream becomes part of the complexion, the blusher coats it. Cream and foundation become beautiful, desirable, melting into your skin. The blusher adds just enough additional color to keep the other two alive. Blusher also makes the rouge last longer, as its powdery consistency lightly coats the skin. These two coloring agents play roles that complement each other greatly.

Use the added blusher after all your other makeup has been applied, when you're ready to reevaluate your rouge. Lightly stroke it over areas covered by the rouge. Then extend it with just a couple of brushstrokes to blend perfectly with the foundation. If some of the color of the cream has disappeared into your skin, as so often happens, the blusher will bring it back. It's a lovely finishing touch.

You may prefer using only the blusher, dispensing with the rouge altogether. In that case I advise using face powder first (and this is the only time I advise you to use it before, not after). It provides a nice finish to the foundation and also helps set the blusher and hold its color longer. Also it will prevent any blotches from appearing when the blusher is applied to foundation that is still moist. With a light brush of face powder on, the blusher will go on more smoothly.

Blusher can be used to add just a hint of color to the forehead if this is one of your good features and you would like to call a bit of attention to it. Again, it should be first lightly powdered—either along the hairline or at the two prominences; you don't want to give it too much of a good thing. Check to make sure that there are no traces of powder in your hair. Then add the blusher with a light little stroke—a feathering, I would say. This is a marvelous, imperceptible accent. A light blushing at the bridge of the nose—never the tip—is lovely too.

Again check your hair for any loose particles of powder. So much of what makes for chic has to do with careful, immaculate grooming, and that means attention to the smallest details. Tiny particles of powder can be easily removed from your hair with a slightly moistened cotton ball or tip of a washcloth. Perfection takes only a little time, effort and attention to attain. Soon your eyes will be trained to notice the slightest deviation. And you'll know just how to correct it.

Cheek Color

Years ago there was only dry rouge in pink, orange, bright red and a blue-red that closely resembled purple! Today you have a total range that runs the gamut from pink to red to orange, with every beautiful, subtle shade in between. You have terrific shades of brick, sepia, brown and tan—tawny, sandy shades that are absolutely delicious. These are colors that make sense—few people really blush to a shade of orange. You blush naturally to a tone that is a flush of your skin's color. The terra cottas, the walnuts, the peach shades are perfect. There is also a wide range of such wine colors as burgundy, colors that make your whole face sparkle.

By looking at your face after coming in from the cold you will see the color you are trying to emulate. And the look you create will be even better than the one nature stamped on you, one that will look just as believable and real as the weather's creation.

The color you choose is also dictated in part by your foundation. Because we are always looking for a total, cohesive look in makeup, foundation and rouge must be compatible. What you want are two products whose casts agree: your foundation and your rouge must work together rather than create an unseemly contrast.

Pale, light foundations go best with wine rouge shades. Burgundies blend best with beige-, yellow- or ivory-based foundations whereas a brick shade would stand out noticeably.

Medium-intensity foundations work with basically any shade or intensity of rouge—no restrictions here.

Dark foundations, those used when you are tan, are enhanced by rouge of a brick, bronze or terra cotta shade—colors that are strong enough to brighten a tanned, or darker, complexion. They add a devastating glow that heightens the sensuous appeal of dark skin.

There are other factors to be considered when selecting a rouge. If you have especially pale skin, you might like to try a great red— cherry red, fire-engine red, Chinese red—the color that nearly white skin blushes to. Brights work exceptionally well on black skin, which needs all the lights of a strong red.

For a more mature woman who uses flattering pinkish-toned foundation, a pink as well as a red rouge is great. Particularly if you wear pastels and neutrals, pink is a good selection and a change from the traditional. There is something about the softness of pink that works magic on the skin, but be sure you are applying enough for a good, healthy glow. Don't be timid and let rouge disappear into the foundation instead of adding that something extra.

I don't think that any woman needs a whole shelf full of rouge jars to create good makeup. For most, an earthy color (names of fruits and nuts, beiges, browns and tawnies) is good for daytime and summertime, plus a wine color for the evening. For those who have a very pale or mature complexion, red and pink.

Face Powder

Although I believe that you can achieve a perfectly fine makeup without face powder, many women wish to include it in their routines. It does provide a wonderful matte finish to a makeup and is good for the "T" zone, where you want a nonshiny look. If you have a shiny nose, by all means powder it. But remember that powder does not belong all over the face. Powder has a tendency to settle into lines and wrinkles, emphasizing them. I never use powder around the eyes, because that area, as well as cheeks and lips, should always look dewy.

Powder, if it is used, must be used intelligently. By that I mean sparingly. Great clouds of powder can not only coat you and your clothes (both unbecoming) but it can also clog pores. Tinted face powder presents another problem—it has a tendency to turn color, becoming yellow or orangey, depending on your skin tones.

Luckily, modern cosmetic laboratories have revolutionized face powder. Today's colorless powder seems spun out of air. Its formula has helped relieve both the clogging and the color-buildup problems. This translucent, colorless powder is the only one I use on my clients and the only one I recommend without hesitation. Colorless powder really means less color, rather than no color. The powder goes on invisibly, but is available in three tones: light, medium and dark. Therefore you only need one shade—a good economic factor. Once you find the right one, you'll never have to change or need any other.

The same fine consistency works for black, Caucasian, Oriental, Indian—any skin tone. It doesn't change the color of your foundation or your rouge. It simply helps set whatever you've used and keeps it nonshiny—a divine invention. This powder comes in two formats, loose and compact. If you are a heavy powder user, I suggest the loose kind; to everyone else, the compact.

For loose powder, a clean puff and cotton balls for removing excess provide for the best method of application. You can use a sponge, moistened and wrung almost dry, to help set the powder.

For compact powder, the best tool is not the puff but the brush. A nice broad brush, such as the one used to apply blusher, will deposit a much lighter dusting of powder than the puff. It can also get into those hard-to-reach corners—the sides of the nose, the corners of the nostrils, places powder should be applied carefully or lightly. When applying around the nose, draw your upper lip over your upper teeth, stretching the area for the moments you need to.

Unfortunately the brush will not work with loose powder; too much powder adheres to the bristles. The compact with its pressed powders is an all-around convenience. It slips into your purse or carrying case without causing you any worry that it might open and spill out. The brush usually comes with it, giving you the proper size you need for the purpose. Just stroke the brush across the pressed powder and you have the right amount ready to apply.

Your powder purchase, whether loose or compact, should last you many years—that's how sparingly it should be used. And although I restrict the areas to which it should be applied, powder does have its purpose and place. When used properly, it acts as a veil against impurities of weather and air pollution. It worked just that way for our grandmothers, who had only powder to use as a total makeup. Remember how soft their cheeks were?

Though powder is a nice finishing touch, rouge is the most important element of this chapter. It's a beautiful step that every woman should enjoy. Wearing a lot of rouge is like having money in the bank.

CHAPTER NINE

A Look at the Eyes

Eyes are the most important feature of the face. When you're communicating with someone, if you're having a conversation, if you're having a meeting, if you're having a fight, if you're flirting, if you're dancing, if you're sharing a meal with someone, you will almost always be looking into each other's eyes.

The person you are with will glance at all of you of course—your hands, your clothes, your hair, your jewelry. But after glimpsing everything else, one always relates to people's eyes. "Looking someone straight in the eye" has become an expression indicating honesty. "To have one's eye on something" means to be aware, to be with it. Especially when two people talk, they look into each other's eyes. Therefore it's very important to have pretty eye makeup. What we have to do for the eyes is decorate them intelligently, always doing what will enhance them and beautify them as much as possible.

If the eyes are small, we try to make them look larger; if they're protruding, we will try to set them back. If the lashes are light and unattractive, we can make them dark and luscious and interesting.

Eye Shadow Colors

Makeup for the eyes should be chosen to *enhance* and not to *match* whatever you are wearing—a mistake that many women make. A green dress does not call for green eye shadow. In fact, I consider green a rather difficult eye shadow color, because it tends to be so blatant. Even if you have *green eyes*, I don't suggest trying to match the shadow. If you look carefully at your eyes you will see that they are not really bright emerald green or sage green or bottle green; the green eye has always a little bit of many colors. It may be chiefly green, but there is brown, there is yellow, there is gray, there is hazel in it. And if you use a really green eye shadow, you *kill* whatever little green you may have in your eyes. To emphasize the green eye it's always better to use a contrasting color, such as plum or gray or brown.

Brown is a fabulous eye-shadow color, but somehow it's always hard for women to believe that brown eye shadow can do more for them than almost any other color. Brown eye shadow may sound drab, but it will actually make it possible for your own eye color, whatever it is, to really show well. Brown eye shadow can be used by almost anybody. A young girl who is just starting to use makeup could easily use a pale doeskin or light tobacco brown or other beige coloring on her lids and look lovely and innocent.

Brown eye shadow brings out the actual color of the eyes, emphasizes the background and gives a very beautiful look to the entire eye area. It's important to create depth, because without depth nothing really stands out. A painter knows that. For example, in painting an apple realistically, the artist gives the impression of its roundness by painting shades that are darker and darker as he approaches the extreme contour of the fruit. Then, where the maximum light hits the apple, there's a white spot which is called the highlight. The same principle works on our faces when we want to emphasize and de-emphasize.

Let's say we want to de-emphasize the brow bone so that the eye becomes more outstanding. In this case the use of brown eye shadow will give the effect of pushing the bone back, highlighting the eye itself. I love to create a look for the eyes that adds *depth* rather than color. This is easily achieved by using a *pale* shade of brown from the bottom of the lid up into the crease, and then a deeper shade from the crease up to the brow. Even the woman with blue eyes who is used to matching her shadow to her eye color may find she achieves a more interesting effect with the use of brown.

In fact, the only woman for whom I would not recommend use of the brown shadow would be the woman whose hair has mostly grayed. Only in her case brown would look drab. It would be much more interesting for her to use some shade of blue, which will do more to perk up the eyes. Gray, such as a beautiful chinchilla, is also very effective. Because they have so much blue in them, the entire range of lavenders are also flattering to gray- and white-haired women.

Blue eyes are also flattered by the contrast of gray or plum. A very dark plum or a reddish brown, such as the copper brown or brick colors, is also very interesting with blue eyes.

Brown eyes can use almost any color and look fine, but you also have to take into consideration the color of your hair. A *brunette* may find that her whole look becomes too dark if she uses dark eye color. Instead, she may want to choose a lovely shade of aqua or turquoise or a pale shade of green or blue or any of the lavender shades, the heathers or the lilacs. They're all very pretty on brown eyes. If this contrasting color is used from the *bottom of the upper lid* up to the crease, then the entire eye area will be enhanced by the use of a rusty brown from the *crease to the brow*. Thus the brunette will have the highlighting of the eye provided by the color closest to it and still achieve depth for the over-all eye area by the use of the brown, not in its darkest but rather in a redder variation, on the upper lid.

For *the brown-eyed* woman with *blond* or *red* hair, a very pretty look can be achieved by the use of a soft teal shade or any shade in the plum family; the heathers or a very subtle sage green will also be correct.

For *black eyes*, whether of a black woman or a Caucasian, I like to use brighter colors but *in a very small amount*. In other words, it shouldn't be the entire lid that is shadowed in blue or gray or turquoise. The color should be used very close to the lashes, both on the top lid, with an eye-shadow applicator, and *under* the bottom lashes, with a pencil of the same color, thus creating an intensity of color but on a *small* surface. For the rest of the lid any pale shade—pale beige, pale pink, pale lilac, pale brown—could go over the entire upper lid area. But the deep color should go only very near the lashes.

The time of day when eye makeup will be worn is very important from the point of view of appropriateness and lighting. Every woman needs a good makeup mirror; bathrooms seldom come equipped with one, and consequently makeup is generally applied in front of the poorly lit mirror of the medicine cabinet that comes with a house or an apartment. Therefore a makeup mirror with an adjustable light is a must.

Even after you have put on your makeup in front of a good mirror, there should be additional checking in the various lights to which you'll be subjected once you go out. If you're going to be out during the day, check your makeup near a window. If you're going out for the evening, use your own living room light as a guide.

In order to obtain the best possible eye makeup results for yourself, you should be aware, first, of all the *formats* available, and then of the techniques for faultless *application*.

Eye Shadow Formats

Eye-shadow coloring comes in several different forms. There is the *cream*, which was developed for its nondrying effects and is made in many very pretty shades. But, alas, it is not long-lasting and often runs into the creases of the lids, becoming very messy-looking, and is therefore impractical for most purposes. There is also a *cream liquid* which comes out of a wand. I feel that these wands tend to apply too much color, and they get coated and tacky after they've been used for a while.

In addition, there are those fat *crayon pencils*, which are one of the newest makeup products. I prefer these for the quick five-minute makeup, for coloring under the bottom lashes, and for lining and shading rather than for over-all application of color. A pencil, even a soft one, is not the kindest thing for use on the delicate eyelid and must be used with the utmost care.

Creamy pressed powder eye shadow is the most perfect form we have today. It can be applied with the fingers, a brush or a sponge. This is not only the most *long-lasting* of all the types of eye shadow but it is the most easily blended, so that when you are wearing more than one shade, it is simple to avoid any demarcation line between them. Since I like the look of a lighter color from the lashes to the crease of the lid and a darker shade from the crease up to the brow, this becomes important for a faultless application.

Eye Shadow Application

Because pressed shadow is the one I prefer, this is the application I want to discuss. However, many of the principles will apply to any format. The color that is to be applied from the roots of the upper lashes to the crease of the lid—a doeskin, for example—should go on first. If you are right-handed, use your left hand to hold the skin of the upper lid taut, pulling slightly toward the temple. Be sure the color gets into the outer corner, where it should be more intense and disappear neatly, blending with the foundation. Should the eye shadow have crumbled or inadvertently been applied where you don't want it, soften it away with a tissue. Shadow of *any* kind tends to collect in the crease and in the inner corner as the day wears on, and it can become quite messy. Also be sure that no shadow has landed where you don't want any, such as on the cheeks or the sides of the nose.

Stroke coppery brown onto the upper lid to the brow, working again toward the outer area. Make the first strokes in the middle of the brow bone, then work the color to the inner corner, then to the outer. Mid-brow is a good place to begin, as the first touch of color on the skin tends to leave the greatest amount. For a wide-eyed look you won't want such intensity at the inner corners.

The coppery brown should not stop precisely at the top of the upper lid beneath the brow. Rather, it should be extended, very subtly and lightly, so that it blends imperceptibly with your foundation. The colors should melt into each other with no telltale line of demarcation showing.

Some women use three different shadow colors to make up the upper lid, but I don't like this. There is no way for three colors to look like anything but three colors. Two are sufficient: one, the lighter, on the lower part of the lid, to highlight the eye, and the deeper shade from the crease to the brow, to make the brow bone recede and bring depth to the eye.

Eye shadow can also be beautifully used underneath the *lower lashes*. For this I like the same color—doeskin in this instance—as that used on the lower part of the upper lid. But rather than have it all around the eye, start it at about the middle of the eye, under the bottom lashes, and work it toward the *outer corner* only. This should be a narrow band of color and can be put on with a *pencil* in a matching shade if your shadow applicator is too thick to give you as fine a line as you would like. Thus, if you consider the eye as an entity, the band of one color will surround it only three-quarters of the way—all of the outline above the eye and half below. This is an extremely pretty effect on many women, but it must be done with infinite care so the result is subtle and refined.

Especially women who wear glasses should take the time to perfect all the procedures for the lower eyelid (including instructions for liner and lashes still to come) because glasses tend to obscure this area and makeup can bring it alive again with added interest.

Again, application must be impeccable, because the makeup will sometimes be magnified by the lenses. If you use nothing, it will look like nothing—blah; but if you use too much, it will look like *much* too much.

Eyeliners

Let's take the matter of *eyeliners* now. One thing should be made very clear at the outset when talking about eyeliners, and that is their purpose. *Eyeliners are meant to make the lashes look thicker.* A hard line of color totally surrounding the eye is unattractive; it looks like what it is— a harsh, obviously painted-on line (nobody was born with it!), a garish smear of color. This is not a flattering, believable look.

But eyeliner properly applied (and it does take a little practice) can achieve a devastatingly soft, sexy look that I love. The first step toward mastering this technique is *Stop worrying about making a perfect line.* What you *do* want is to get the liner as close to the roots of the upper-lid lashes as possible. A tiny-tipped brush comes with *cake eyeliner;* use it after the cake has been wetted. Or you can use the *automatic eyeliner* if you prefer. It also comes in liquid form, which needs a brush, but with the cake you have much more control of the amount of liner that you get on the brush. That makes proper application much easier, because the cake dries quickly, whereas the liquid tends to get thick after it's applied.

The liner can be applied as a continuous line or even as a series of dots or dashes, as I suggested in "Makeup in Minutes." In any case, you now have the liner on, almost from corner to corner of the upper eyelid, hugging the lashes. Now, quickly before it dries com-

pletely, with a slightly wider sable-type brush, deliberately *smudge* the eyeliner. Smudge it slightly, clean off the brush, smudge it again, apply a little more liner, and smudge just a few times until you achieve a smoky, soft effect, the liner blurred from its straight line, and you will have gotten a subtle, lash-thickening look that is the most stupendous kind of flattery for the eye. And it is so subtle, no one can really see that it's there. But the *effect* is there, and that is what lovely makeup is about.

Now when you lower your lids to look at something on your desk or to read a menu, the effect is soft, not startling. Just contrast that with the appearance of the thin, hard, dark line painted so unnaturally across your lids. You have added depth and mystery to your eyes, not another product sitting on top of your skin.

The same devastating look can be continued under the *lower lid*, but with a different application technique. With the very point of the tiny eyeliner brush *paint three or four dots* at the roots of the lower lashes, starting at the outer corner and going about to the center of the eye. Then, with your *fingertip* or a *cotton swab*, touch all the dots and *smudge* again. When you add your mascara you will look as if you have the thickest, fullest lashes in the world.

Eyeliner can also be *pencil*, and here, before we get to mascara and lashes, is another way to use the pencil liner. Use a pencil in a color such as skipper blue, and holding the eye area taut with the fingers, pencil in the rim just above the lashes with a soft, light line. The blue will be practically indistinguishable, but the *whites of your eyes* will look clear and bright and whiter than they ever have!

The Brows

The pencil, in the color closest to your own, is great for *brows*. The first tool to use is a brow *brush*, brushing upward over the arch. This will show you where the stray hairs are that should be tweezed out. I don't like the idea of drastically reshaping a brow, but I do like the brows to be light rather than heavy. A heavy brow limits the eye, closes it in, constricts and narrows an area that should be a projection of infinity. Remember the eyes that men could drown themselves in?

Tweezing should always be followed by an application of astringent or alcohol and a rich cream or moisturizer over the entire tweezed and surrounding areas. This is a time when your face needs extra conditioning and some pacifying. The assault of the tweezer leaves it wanting to be pampered. Never follow a tweezing with a makeup, as the minute openings left by tweezing can get clogged by makeup. Plucking is a rather jarring experience for those tiny pores, and they need immediate care and comfort, not an onslaught of products that would at that time only irritate. Kindness to your face is important—in this instance and always.

Brows should be lightly arched, never exaggerated. After brushing them up, use your pencil to make *short, hairlike strokes* where necessary to fill in the sparser areas. Never draw a single continuous line on the brow. This is totally unnatural and results in a hard, menacing, most unattractive look. Any penciling-in that is done should imitate the actual little hairs of the brow.

I have gotten terrific results with *bleaching* the brows. This can be done when the shape of the brow is fine but the color is too dark for the face. My most famous example of this technique is Sophia Loren. Of course she always had a strong, wonderful face, but lightening her brows made her truly unforgettable. It softened her look.

Compare her pictures before and after I started the bleaching, in 1963. Her naturally dark brows conflicted with the strong lines of her face. They kept those marvelous eyes from really projecting as they should. I have found that bleaching the brows not only opens the eye area but that sometimes the entire face takes on a newer, refreshed aspect.

Unnoticeable brows are a very natural thing. Consider those beings in nature who have the most riveting, commanding eyes. Birds. The great cats. *They have no brows at all.* The eyes of the lion, those great golden orbs that can transfix you even in a photograph, are completely open, unshadowed by brows. Now, I'm not suggesting that this would be a correct look for most women. There can be something remarkably attractive about the human eyebrow. But in most cases, which is to say on most faces, the brows should definitely be de-emphasized.

Look at yourself in the mirror. If your brows seem too emphatic, too heavy or dark for your face, then by all means consider having a professional cosmetician bleach them for you. It's a very simple procedure, but one that should be done *for* you and with the proper materials and equipment.

You may also like the way you look with your brows *brushed up*, as I suggest they should be before tweezing. Brows brushed up also take the line away from the eye, again *opening* the area. Look at portraits of ladies in Renaissance paintings. See how light and thin the brows were. What expressions of serenity were achieved that way, and what attention was brought to the eye! Those eyes look as though they could go on forever. Remember what I said about extending the eye-shadow color on the upper part of the lid, past the outer corner of the eye, blending toward the temples? That is a great way to extend the eye and achieve this beautiful look.

The Lashes

We are now ready to give the finishing touch to the eye area—grooming the lashes. I love the look of great, black, sweeping lashes and the use of lots and lots of mascara to make it come true. I think it's difficult to use too much mascara. Unlike the brows, whose heaviness may constrict the eyes, the surrounding fringe of lashes

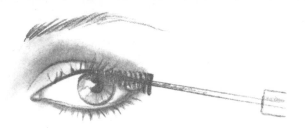

becomes lovelier as it becomes thicker. Great, sweeping lashes are enormously flattering to the eyes and indeed to the entire face. I love to see lashes that seem to radiate almost in a starlike effect, out from the eye, brushing almost against the cheek.

Almost all mascara today is applied with the wandlike applicator, whose top is a brush and whose bottom is a well holding the mascara. It's a terrific tool, in that it does away with the smearing and uncertainty of those old tiny brush-and-cake sets. This is easy:

Holding the lid down, brush on mascara, on the top of the lashes *first from the roots to the tips*. Then, with the eye open, brush on another coat from bottom to top. This puts two coats on the upper lashes. Then do the lower lashes, from the roots outward, on the upper surface only. By this time the first coats on the upper lashes should be dry, and you can apply second coats. This should give you thick, lush, long, lashes.

For an even fuller effect, such as you might want in the evening, carefully brush some *baby powder* on the lashes before applying the mascara. Or you might want to go as far as putting on a third coat of mascara. This should certainly provide sufficient buildup to give even sparse lashes a wonderful fullness.

Buying and Applying False Eyelashes

For those women who want even more emphasis, with *false eye-lashes*, I will outline how that can best be done, although I must stress that I am no longer very fond of them. Their application requires a great deal of time and patience to produce an effect that mascara can amply and easily provide. They must be trimmed and fitted to you so that they look real, and putting them on properly, really properly, is only accomplished in one way: lash by individual lash. Most women who wear them use the strip lashes, and the application must be perfectly done. So if you insist, this is the way to do it:

The first thing to be careful about is *color*. The preferable shade, no matter what color your own lashes are, is *charcoal* or *dark brown*. Black lashes are much too hard and phony-looking. After they're applied they will be mascara'ed along with your natural ones, and the color will even out.

Now the lashes *must* be trimmed carefully to fit you. The lashes should not go from corner to corner. If they do, it will be painful, if not impossible, to close your eyes. Look at your own lashes carefully. The little hairs do not start growing exactly at the inner corner of the eye. They start perhaps a millimeter away, and that is where the false lashes should begin as well.

Most lashes sold come with their own adhesive; if not, you can buy surgical glue at any drugstore.

Before applying the lashes, coat your own with one application of mascara. Then, looking straight into the mirror, you're ready to begin. Place the strip of lashes over your own, pushing down until they touch. Then press the strip down on the lid, where the eyeliner may be.

Then apply another coat of mascara, brushing it on both the false lashes and your own. If you have applied the proper amount of glue, the lashes should be well set in place, very comfortably blending with your own. At this point you can apply still another coat of the mascara if you think you need it.

If you have the problem of the ends popping up from the lid, then you have either not used sufficient glue or permitted it to dry before having pressed the lashes into place. If this happens, take a *tooth-pick* and dip one end of it into the glue. Touch it very carefully to the corner of your lid where the lash belongs. You need only the smallest pinpoint of glue. Then with tweezers push the lash back and it will stay. Now apply the second coat of mascara, brushing the lashes together so that you can *feel confident* that they are going to stay.

Check in your mirror between each step of the application, always looking down into it so that you can see how you look when you close your lids. This is the giveaway time, when imperfect application always shows up. If you have put the strip close enough to your own roots, if mascara and eyeliner are properly applied, then there should be no demarcation to announce you're using false eyelashes.

It is equally important to check the eyes against each other. The application must be true to the symmetry of the face and the relationship of the eyes. You can't have the lashes going in wildly different directions. This is one of the reasons that application of false eyelashes to the bottom lid is so tricky and that I don't recommend it for any but the most accomplished.

Open and close your eyes several times, rapidly, as a final test. Touch the lashes lightly to make sure that they won't be falling off. This touchability, this believability, is the most essential element in good makeup application, not only for the eyes but for everywhere. You should always touch, pat, massage your face with loving-kindness. You should not be afraid to risk scratching the surface because you've got an inch-thick coat of paint on, like a Japanese Kabuki mask. You should be able to touch every area of the face without fear of smudging, except for the lips. (The lipstick formulations today are so creamy they will always "run.") Just touch the very ends of the lashes to prove to yourself that they are on correctly.

Once you perfect the technique of applying upper lashes, you may want to attempt to do the lower ones. I feel that this is not at all necessary and can have disastrous results. Lower lashes must look natural. Improperly applied lower lashes could look rather freakish. When experimenting, keep your eyes very steady and wide open. Stare right into the mirror. Hold the strip of false lashes with the tweezer. Go under your own with the false ones and pat the glued strip gently in place. (Individual extra lashes here will require a great knack, so be careful!)

I feel that usually it is easier for you to follow my directions and makeup tips than it is for me to describe them. Even things that sound extremely complicated when you read them become very clear and simple once you pick up your tools and get to work. But this is not true here. Putting on any lashes, especially lower ones, is a difficult job at best. You must really be convinced of their necessity before you take the time and effort it requires.

Night Eyes

Many women want to glamorize their eyes at *night* with the use of highlighter and frosted shades. If used sparingly, they may work, although to me the pastel or the neutrally shadowed eye is much more flattering and *believable*.

Instead of frosted colors, which can give you a rather hard look if seen up close, use *more* of the shadow that you have found to be most flattering to you and that you usually wear. This added amount might be all the touch of extra you need. Of course, lots and lots of mascara.

For a lovely finishing touch, try this. After you apply the blue eyeliner to the rim of the lower lid, as described before, use a tiny amount of *white pencil* just where the blue stops at the outer corner and the skin starts. This is an empty space that can be made even more emphatically an opening for the whole eye area.

I think that these impeccable finishing touches do much more for the eyes than all the flashy iridescents and frosteds. One will never look cheap by putting on a greater amount of, say, brown eye shadow, but the garish colors can be instant destruction of any chic or femininity you may have otherwise achieved. It saddens me to see so many women misuse makeup when proper application could really be helpful to them.

Bright, beautiful eyes have very much the same appeal that precious gems do. If you mount them with a great deal of fussy detail around them, you are taking away from the importance of the gem. On the other hand, a simple setting emphasizes the gem and makes it even more outstanding. That is the frame of reference I would like you to develop for your eyes.

CHAPTER TEN

A Word on the Lips

The mouth is a feature that does so much all by itself. The mouth is expressive: we use it to talk, to laugh, to smile, to kiss, to grimace. It shows approval and disapproval. We broaden it to grin, contract it when we pucker, distend it when we pout (which I hope is not often). There is no other feature that is quite so mobile; it doesn't need much help from us. I would almost say that the more you use your mouth, the less makeup it needs.

Many women are unhappy about their mouths. The best thing for them to do, and for everyone, is to color the mouth simply and lightly and to play up the other features. To me the most attractive part of the face is from the nose up. I pay much more attention to the eyes, as a makeup artist and as a man, than I do to the mouth. All that is necessary for the mouth is that it shows sufficiently, that it is present in the geography of the face. One should never feel overpowered by the mouth.

In keeping with my philosophy of a natural approach to makeup, I believe you should follow the natural contour of your mouth. Using lipstick to make the mouth look either fuller or smaller is one of the worst makeup mistakes a woman can make. Worrying about your mouth is an exaggerated worry; recontouring your mouth is exaggerated makeup. I'm against both.

It is true that a number of tricks are used in photography to enhance a model's mouth, but these are impractical in everyday situations. You are constantly using your mouth, talking and eating away lipstick. A corrective application would be gone in the first bite of breakfast.

There is, however, one trick that will work rather well for a thin or weak upper lip. With a very fine brown pencil lightly touch up the points of the center of your upper lip, the "M" we all have. With a fine cotton swab blend the pencil into your lip, softening any hardness at the contour. When you add your lipstick the brown won't show, but its effect will, adding body to the lip without showing any effort.

Remember that the mouth should never dominate the face; it should never be drawn in falsely to look like a caricature instead of two beautiful lips.

Trying to make too little of your lips is as bad as its reverse. Both are signals that tell everyone you are self-conscious about your mouth. I have noticed that black women who may be very full-lipped often try coloring only halfway within the contour of their lips; I disapprove of this. Any woman who wants to minimize the size of her mouth should do so inconspicuously. This is best achieved by using a gloss only or a very light shade of lipstick or no lipstick at all. Try all three methods to see which will be best for you.

As long as I've mentioned the possibility of wearing no lipstick, I should discuss it in regard to everyone. Although this practice was in vogue several years ago, and did work terrifically for some women, I was never really fond of it. For minimizing the lips, yes; for very young faces, yes; for some great faces, to dramatize magnificent bone structure and emphasize the eyes, yes; for every woman, no. Too often no lipstick tells the person looking at you that you have simply forgotten or tried to erase your mouth; it is not a correct look. Fortunately, the cosmetics industry countered this trend with gloss—for a natural shine without color. Many women still use it alone.

Often the question depends on individual preference. I feel that most women could use the little bit of help that lipstick does provide. It's a cosmetic that's fairly easy to use, and none other has as wide a range of colors from which to choose. The possibilities for experimenting are endless and a lot of fun. You can even create your own colors by blending two prepackaged ones. A marvelous new shade of lipstick puts a touch of color into a dull day, a monotonous situation, a tired face. A new lipstick can give an instant lift that many women will find therapeutic. What can put a bright and instant smile on a face if not lipstick?

Of all the makeup products in use today lipstick disappears fastest from the face—its only drawback. But its great advantage is the moisturizing effect most new formulations have on lips. Old lipstick formulations—those dark purples and garish oranges of the twenties and thirties—were practically indelible, as they were made from harsh, harmful dyes. Today's formulas are softer, creamier, lovelier, as are today's colors. But how fast it disappears!—faster than last season's fashions. Yet every time you put it on again during the day or night you will add to its beneficial, conditioning effect.

At times the lips require even more soothing protection. Like the rest of your body, they are exposed to wind, cold, heat, and other drying elements such as air conditioning, which can all cause peeling, cracking and chapping. Lipstick's creamy formulations help, but you may want to supplement their effectiveness by using other products. An eight-hour cream has marvelous moisturizing qualities. Lip lubricants, such as pomade sticks, will help keep the lips smooth. Lips need a great deal of lubrication; use pomade or moisturizers as often as you can, even when you're at home, even when you have no other makeup on. An especially good time is when you're using a mask.

Application

Putting on lipstick is a very simple thing. You can, if you wish, use a pencil to outline the lips before coloring in with a stick. If you do, be sure that the pencil is as close as possible in color to the lipstick. You don't want any contrast between them. The pencil can be especially helpful if you have a problem with lipstick running into the tiny lines in the skin above the upper lip. The pencil will prevent this spreading.

If you forgo the pencil, simply apply lipstick first to the contour of

your lips and then fill in. Fill the entire area, blot with a tissue and apply again to help set the color.

You can use a lipstick brush for a velvety smooth application and a more professional look. The brush tip, being finer than that on the lipstick, will give you a nice degree of control once you get used to handling it. Brushstrokes agree with the texture of the lips as the artist's brush agrees with the canvas—a lovely approach and a helpful tool.

For some women, a light coat of face powder before the lipstick goes on may help the color to last longer. For others, often the more you apply, the faster it disappears. It all depends on your lips—their texture and condition. Unfortunately, you can rarely do without freshening lip color—always in thin, smooth applications.

Color

Color is a very important consideration. I love color that is compatible with the rest of the face. You do not need seventy different shades to match everything in your wardrobe. I like a light color for the brightest hours of the day; a pale, murky shade for a no-lipstick look; two or three brighter shades for evening.

While I don't believe in matching what you wear on your mouth to what you wear on your body, there must be a color compatibility. Lipstick, unlike eye shadow, must be coordinated with your clothes; they should never clash.

Bright colors first. If you are wearing green you can wear orange and brown shades.

For red I suggest a complementary red or brownish shade. Avoid pinks.

Light, bright or dark blues in clothing go very well with the clear reds, pinks and stronger colors. The one to avoid here is orange.

For an orange outfit, however, you should have at least a suggestion of orange in your lipstick. It doesn't have to be bright; it could be a lovely shade of mandarin or apricot or coral. A pink or red—especially one with blue tones—will clash awfully.

Brown takes very well to shades of coral and a wide range of pinks and reds. All of the tawny colors work well here.

Lavender and purple shades can take light pinks or wonderful burgundies. Brown burgundy is good with formal haute couture, as are all the smoky shades.

For black clothes practically any bright color will do. It should be strong enough to balance this strongest of all neutrals.

Whites, bones and pastels work best with misty, rosy shades of lipstick, which are flattering and can be worn by almost everyone.

When we think of marvelous lips we think of such words as "luscious," "wet," "kissable." The suggestion of something infinitely desirable and romantic should be there, and that's why I don't like dark, dark shades of lipstick at any time. Reds, pinks, corals—they're all so much more beautiful on you.

As I hinted briefly, you can create custom colors yourself—a trick I learned from Elizabeth Arden herself. We in the cosmetics industry can create an endless array of colors, but once the color is set, that is it. But you can go on to create infinite combinations by applying two shades and blotting them together to form one.

You can create your very own shade which no one can duplicate, your very own exclusive. There's another advantage as well: color correcting. Often when you buy a beautiful lipstick color that looks wonderful in the tube, it turns out to be wrong on you. By changing the tone slightly you can perfect the color. A beige or pink will lighten a red that looks too bright. A brown shade can tone down a pink that is too pink. In fact, any lip color can be easily modified.

The application of two lipsticks is no more difficult than applying one. Always put on the most important color first, the color whose statement is stronger. The second, modifying color goes over it. The first color takes on your lips; the second sets and corrects it—a finishing touch.

Gloss

I love the look of gloss. The shiny mouth is always most appealing, most attractive. Unfortunately, gloss wears away with the lipstick under it and needs frequent reapplication. But the appealing look it gives is well worth the effort. A tip from models is to use gloss on the ridge of the bottom lip, the area least used when talking. Keeping it looking shiny there is less of a problem.

The gloss I use most often on my clients is a clear, colorless shiner. It works on the same principle as the translucent face powder: it doesn't cause any color buildup no matter how often it's applied. It keeps the mouth moist and luscious, as it fights off the lines and cracks that often plague the lips.

Gloss works well during active sports when you may not want to bother with lipstick. It goes well with casual clothes and casual occasions. It offers good protection against sun and wind, especially for the woman who prefers going without lipstick altogether.

Because so many women do use gloss alone, it is made in a great range of shades as well as the colorless varieties. Some sound more like delicious desserts than cosmetics—plum, strawberry, peach. A woman's mouth *should* suggest a sweet, delectable treat.

A truly wonderful lip product is the new gloss and lipstick in one, giving you only one thing to apply, and the choice of shades is growing each day.

All glosses are available in easy-to-carry forms—little pots, tubes and sticks. I prefer the tubes, from which you squeeze out a small amount onto a finger for quick application.

And there you have a simple approach to smooth, soft, shiny lips and the way to use a little to make you look a lot better.

Part IV

DISTILLATIONS

CHAPTER ELEVEN

A Talk with Teenagers

A girl's first experience with makeup usually comes long before she's in her teens. As a little girl playing "dress-up" with her mother's clothes, most likely one of the first things she reached for was a shiny tube of lipstick. Can you remember how *you* looked with that first bright-red *glob* smeared all over your mouth? Certainly it was incongruous, even though at the time it was quite daring and a lot of fun! But there is a message for you today, when you are ready to start wearing makeup quite regularly, that you can get from that little girl.

If you have read the other chapters in this book you already know that lipstick is one of the *last*, not the first, things to reach for. The things that should come first are those I want most to talk to you about. Learning to apply lipstick or foundation or rouge or any other cosmetic is relatively easy. It's what must come before all of that that is so important to you, to the beauty you want to develop and to the beauty you want to keep for all of your life.

Beauty in a woman always starts with her *skin*, and it is never too early to start. Your skin is really your most important asset, now and later on. As you get older your features assume the look you are going to have as an adult, and you may find that you have been blessed with the kind of bone structure that makes a face truly memorable. But during the teens that bone structure stays pretty much hidden. Your face tends to retain some of the roundness of childhood, and those high cheekbones and other elegant traits you admire in the magazine models you see are obscured by what is called "baby fat." Even the slimmest girls have this puffiness to some degree. If you ever come across pictures of Jackie Onassis taken during her teens and even into her twenties, you can see how round her face was. The chic, tailored, *bony* look she is famous for didn't really develop until much later in her life.

That lack of structure makes the skin so much more important, because a beautiful, clear complexion must carry the double burden. And even when the other features do develop, it will still be the skin that provides the *basis* for every aspect of facial beauty. It is hard for you at present to think of what your skin will be like ten or twenty or thirty years from now, but those days will come, and the care you give your skin *now* will pay you beauty rewards for the rest of your life.

It is very easy, very necessary, and very rewarding to get started on a beauty routine that you can follow for the rest of your life. The steps are basically the same—allowing for differences in skin types— for every woman in the world. Your terrific advantage is that you can start *now* while your skin is at its youngest and *best*. You don't have to suffer the anguish of so many older women who have learned the hard way that the calendar cannot be turned back and that it is too late for all the things they should have been doing at your age. And once we have gotten the essentials of skin care taken care of, we can get on to the much more exciting business of makeup and how you should use it.

The two most important elements of skin care are: cleansing and moisturizing. These procedures should become part of your everyday life, routines as automatic as brushing your teeth and combing your hair. Cleaning and moisturizing are absolute necessities for every type of skin. How you clean can even help determine *what* kind of skin you're going to have.

That doesn't mean that there is a way to change dry skin to oily or vice versa. It does mean that proper skin care can help prevent the breakouts and blemishes that plague most teenagers. It does mean that the dryness that comes to attack many women even in their twenties can be pushed back, delayed a little longer. It does mean that the velvety smoothness of young skin can be retained for more than the usual number of years.

I'm sure that when I mention the beauty of a young complexion, many of you wonder whom I may be talking about—the lucky girl in your class, perhaps, who hasn't got a single pimple or blackhead to worry about, but surely not you, already prone to these problems and not knowing what to do about them. Well, I honestly feel that even with all the complexion problems that you may have, your skin itself is still young and worth caring for, and that those problems do have some solutions. Part of the solution may be found in the cleansing and another part in what you are feeding your skin.

The first thing we must do when we discuss cleaning the complexion properly is to separate different skin types and treat them accordingly. Let's talk about dry, normal, and oily skin types, and the combination types that are also quite common.

Oily Skin

As soon as a girl reaches her teens she should begin to use a milky liquid cleanser to wash her face with. There are dozens of these on the market to choose from. They clean your face in a way that soap and water never can. We all know the nice feeling you get from washing your face with soap and water, but believe me, this feeling is more psychological than anything else. Soap-and-water washing is only superficial and cannot get deep down into the pores, where skin trouble starts.

The cleansing lotions are composed of ingredients that are especially formulated to penetrate the skin surface. They contain humectants and oils that go into the pores, clean them out, and come back to the surface again. Don't be afraid that because of these ingredients, the cleanser will add to the problem you already have— oiliness. The cleanser is not meant to *stay* on your skin. It should be applied in a rotating motion all over the face, especially in the places where dirt and oils tend to accumulate. Then as soon as it's done its work it should be quickly and thoroughly removed with warm water, splashed on generously.

Because you have oily skin, it wouldn't hurt to use a little soap and water after the cleansing lotion, but only lightly and for only as long as your complexion stays oily. Once your skin starts to show signs of dryness, stop the soap entirely.

I know that for all of your life you have been hearing your parents tell you to go and wash your face. You grew up on soap and water and now suddenly you're being told to stop using it, either entirely or not so often. But this is actually a change in your life, just like so many others that are occurring because you're growing up. You're probably wearing much different clothes now from those you wore when you were a little girl—except for the blue jeans of course!—and you've started to or soon will wear makeup. This big change in your life requires others. The cleansing lotion is one of the most important.

Not only as protection against all the dirt and pollution and other nuisances that we are required to wash our faces for but also because of the changes going on inside your body *and* the use of makeup, the cleansing lotion becomes a must. And although dry skin is not your problem now, it will be someday in the future. Constant use of soap can only bring that sad day closer.

Soap simply cannot clean the way the lotion can, and it is possible for you to check that out for yourself. Wash the way you usually do, with soap and water, then rotate some milky cleanser on your cheek with a cotton ball or bit of tissue. You'll see all the dirt that the soap left behind.

There is, however, one type of soap that is somewhat beneficial. In any drugstore or department store you can buy really delicious nonalkaline, clear, see-through soaps that are very fresh and pleasant to use. They are good in the tub, and if you have to use any soap on your face, I prefer that you select one of these, as it will help counter oiliness. These soaps are usually a soft amber color and have none of the added ingredients that so many of the commercially advertised soaps contain, ingredients that are really not good for your face. Detergents are for your laundry, and deodorants are for your underarms; you don't really want them rubbed into your face.

Okay, now you're convinced, and your washing routine starts with the use of a liquid, milky cleansing lotion. What next? As I mentioned earlier, the cleanser is not meant to stay on the skin; it is an agent for removing dirt, and the sooner it's gone from the skin, the better. After rinsing it off with water, you will want to make doubly sure that no traces of it remain; after all, it has just brought up the dirt from your pores, why have that hanging around on your skin? The next step is to use another very important product, with two important duties to perform for your face: a *skin* (not cleansing) *lotion*, or *mild astringent*. This product is also liquid, but it is usually clear, unlike the milky cleanser, which, as the name implies, is white and opaque. (The cleansing lotion looks like milk, the skin lotion, or astringent, looks like water.)

The first thing that the skin lotion does is to get rid of any traces of the cleanser that might be left on your face. It is *second-step* cleaning, and you know there is no such thing as being *too* clean. Then, the skin lotion helps to counteract the oiliness of your skin. For you I recommend an astringent type of lotion that is perhaps 50 percent alcohol. While this would be too much for your older sister or friend with dry skin, it is excellent for you. It will help close the large pores that are usually part of the oily-skin problem, so that dirt is less likely to get in and cause breakouts. It will also keep you from looking quite so shiny quite so soon after cleaning. Again, as you get a little older and the oiliness is somewhat lessened, switch to a less drying skin lotion. The skin, especially young skin, is delicate. It has to last a lifetime, battling all sorts of things that aren't any good for it. Your beauty routine should include only those things that *are* good, that are beneficial to you and your skin.

And speaking of good, there is nothing as good for you as *moisturizer*. Next to cleansing, using moisturizer is the most important thing you can do for your skin. Even if your skin is very oily you need it, because moisturizer adds to the amount of *water* that your skin requires. Water and oil should not be confused. It is not only the dry skin that requires moisturizing, it is *every* skin.

Moisturizer is a bridge: it is the connection between skin care and makeup—that is, it is the last thing to go on the face after the other skin-care products have been used; it is the first thing to go on before you apply foundation or any other cosmetic. It finishes one process, the care; it begins the other, the beauty. I can think of no other single product that is more important for your face.

Since to combat the oil in your skin I have suggested using a good alcohol-based astringent, the need for the moisturizer is even greater. The astringent will have stripped some essential oils from your face which must be replaced. The moisturizer will do that for you. Unbelievable as it may sound, overly oily skin still needs some oils.

What I recommend for your face is a very light moisturizer, one that is absorbed very quickly into the skin. Use less coverage on the nose and other areas that are oiliest, but use *some* everywhere.

Now we must get on to making the routine really a routine. Certainly every night before you go to bed you should follow these three steps: use cleansing lotion, skin lotion (astringent) and, finally, moisturizer. If you have time to do this in the morning as well, that's all to the good. As a matter of fact, the more time during the day that you can give to your beauty routine, the better.

Dry Skin

If you have skin that flakes easily, that doesn't feel quite as smooth as you want it to, then you probably have dry skin. It has a duller cast than that of your friend whose oily skin looks shiny all the time. Even with dry skin, however, you may have that shiny nose. What it means is that some areas of your face will have to be treated somewhat differently from others.

But don't worry that the treatment is going to be complicated or difficult for you to keep up with. Really, it's not. The beauty routine that I want you to follow will take only a few moments of your day, but will give you beautiful rewards for now, and for the rest of your life. In the time that it would take you to watch a television commercial you can be following the steps that will lead you to a beautiful complexion, with admired, glowing skin, the basis for good looks in any woman.

Those steps are the same for everyone, as I've just explained to that shiny-faced friend. They consist of cleansing, freshening, and moisturizing. Dry skin means forgetting about using soap on your face and stepping into the wonderful world of adult beauty products. It means preparing your face for both makeup and its careful removal.

Soap is very bad for dry skin because it has many ingredients that will cause even further dryness, and more quickly. Since drying is one of the most *aging* factors to be considered in treating the skin, you need to be very much aware of everything that you use on your face.

That is why I want you to stop using soap entirely. It is too alkaline, which means that it will rob you of your own supply of skin lubricants and moisturizers, the ones that nature gave you. What we want are products that sink deeper into your skin than soap can anyway, that go deeper into the pores to lift out the dirt that has accumulated there, and do not rob you of precious oils and moisture in the process.

For these reasons I love to recommend the use of milky cleansing lotions. If you have read the previous section, you know that I made the same suggestion for oily skin. That's because this product is formulated for *all* skin types—yours, your friend's, even the so-called normal skin. (By the way, it's the same product your mother should be using too!)

You should buy a milky cleansing lotion that is light and creamy, that you can work into your skin easily with light, rotating motions of your fingertips. If you prefer, you can use the cleansing lotion with a washcloth, making sure that it is damp and *completely* clean. Otherwise you're rotating old dirt back into your face.

The lotion should be nongreasy, and it should remain on the skin only as long as it takes you to quickly whip the dirt out of your pores. Then gently *tissue it off*, removing all traces from your skin.

Now the face is clean and ready for the next step, which is the use of a *skin lotion*, or *freshener*. Don't confuse the two lotions. The cleansing lotion that I described for you first is used first, and *only for cleaning*. The skin lotion has a totally different function, that of toning and refining the skin. It also insures that all of the cleansing lotion has been removed from the skin. This is extremely important for two reasons. First, remember that the milky lotion is carrying *out* dirt particles from inside the pores. You certainly don't want those staying on your face. Then, the cleaning ingredients in that lotion are somewhat drying themselves—not enough to cause worry if you clean all of it off with the freshener—but again, not something that you want sitting on top of your skin.

In addition to removing all the cleansing lotion and toning the complexion, the skin lotion, or freshener, also restores the skin to its proper pH factor. That means it is at the best level for receiving anything else that goes on it, whether it's makeup or moisturizer (which we'll get to in a minute). The pH factor represents the balance of acidity and alkalinity that enables the skin to fight off germs and perform its other functions.

The proper skin lotion, or freshener, for dry skin is one that doesn't contain such drying elements as alcohol. It will be mildly astringent and won't take away the natural lubricants in your skin that it needs so much.

As a bonus, I think you will just *love* the nice fresh way the lotions make your skin feel, smell and look. One of the really terrific things about building your way to beauty is that the products you use to achieve your goal can be pleasurable in themselves if you are open to look at them that way.

The third great step in face care is the use of the *moisturizer*. It's an absolute must for all complexions, but extra important for dry skin. In a way, everything that I have advised you to do so far is really in order to *prepare* the skin to receive as much benefit as possible from the use of the moisturizer.

What moisturizer does: It *helps* the skin to retain all of the moisture possible, giving the complexion a fresh, dewy look, acting as a deterrent to flaking and keeping lines from appearing prematurely.

Because it is so important, moisturizers are made in many different formulas, so that everyone can find the one that is right for her skin type and attractive and suitable for her purposes. When you are using the moisturizer as the first step in makeup application, you want one that is light in texture and easy to apply evenly as a makeup base.

The types that I like most for dry skin are the truly strongly performing moisturizers, either one with a frothy, whipped-cream kind of consistency that is rather light, or a thick emulsion that will really create a film of protection for the skin. This product is great for not only the dry but for the very delicate skin that many girls have and naturally want very much to protect. I like a product that forms this film of protection that can last all day, shielding the skin from the effects of weather and pollution. Delicate skin is not necessarily dry skin, but it may have some of the same needs for proper protection, and the same products may work very well for both.

As I mentioned to you before, the skin's pH factor is restored with the help of the skin lotion (your second step), which does not have to be repeated after applying the moisturizer. Make sure that the moisturizer is evenly smoothed over your face, whether or not you are going to put foundation over it. If your nose is oily, as happens so often even with dry skin, use *less* moisturizer there than you do on the rest of your face, but use at least one thin covering coat.

Cleanser. Freshener. Moisturizer. That's it—three simple steps to skin care. This routine should be followed by you every single night of your life. In the morning, at least rinse with clear water, saturate and use a cotton ball with freshener, and dab on a little moisturizer. If you *can* do the full routine in the morning as well, and other times during the day, I know that you will be well rewarded for your efforts. The steps you take now will show results forever.

Normal Skin

What we call normal skin is that which doesn't have all of the problems of the other two types. It does not show the shininess (except maybe on the nose) or the large pores of oily skin, nor does it tend to flake and crack the way dry skin does. Yet this skin needs all the care and protection that the others do, but of a slightly different sort.

All skins need cleaning—that's basic. Cleansing lotion is much better for you than soap. Normal skin will in time tend to become dry with age, and the proper care now will help delay the change. Soap will speed up the drying process that *every* skin type wants to avoid. The same milky cleansing lotion that I recommend for problem skins should be used for the care of normal skin as well. The lotion is more gentle than any soap can be, and it cleans more deeply. Young skin is delicate skin and needs babying as it grows up.

Cleansing lotion should be rotated by the fingertips or applied with a clean washcloth, very gently, into the skin. Rinse it off quickly with splashes of water. Then, when it is almost but not quite dry, take step two, the *freshener*.

For normal skin this should be a *skin* lotion of about 30 percent alcohol. This is mildly astringent and acts as a tonic for your face.

Follow that with your *moisturizer*—step three. For normal skin I suggest a medium-concentration moisturizer, always in fluid form. No cream for you. Always *blot* the moisturizer after applying it.

This is so that your makeup will not run. Use smaller amounts on your nose if it tends to get shiny. The easiest way to do that is to spread the moisturizer (see the chapter on skin care for exact application instructions), either with your fingers or a sponge, from the inner part of the cheeks out toward the temples. Cover the forehead and chin. Do the nose last, with the little amount of the fluid that is left. If you start with the nose first, it will get the greatest, not the least, amount of concentration.

There you have it, your three steps to skin beauty: cleansing lotion, skin lotion (or freshener) and moisturizer. As I said, the three steps are the same for all skin types, all ages, all sorts of women everywhere. The great advantage of youth is that this simple procedure can be started *now*, at the very beginning of your adult life, and can help keep your skin as young-looking as possible for as long as possible.

For, no matter how anxious you are to grow up, you will always want your skin looking young.

Beauty for Everybody

Now we have discussed the different approaches necessary for the different skin types, and we can start to talk about the other parts of the beauty program, in which the rules are the same for everyone. If you have begun the routine I outlined, you may have started noticing changes in your skin already. Once you start, it doesn't take long to see some results. The products you use are part of your introduction to womanhood and, I think, one of the nicest parts. Using these products will help your skin and help you to realize that you, and your life, are getting a little more complicated now! Soap becomes a thing of the past, for your face at any rate, something you've outgrown, just as you've outgrown dolls or other interests you had as a child, which seem childish to you now. Now you are into the wonderful world of beauty, and I really want to make it wonderful for you. You can help make this discovery for yourself by learning to enjoy the things that only a few years ago you were too young for.

Don't look at your beauty routine as a boring necessity. See it instead as the truly feminine and *feminizing* process it is. Enjoy doing it, and enjoy what *it* does for you. For example, certain foods that we are told are good for us (more about that later too!) are very boring to eat. Many of the things that do us good are less interesting and likable than the fun things we just do to enjoy ourselves. Learning to deal with all of that is part of growing up, what we call discipline. But beauty and beauty care aren't like that. The products that make you look good are in pretty packages, they are feminine and good-smelling.

I think every woman, at every age, should love to pamper herself, to enjoy her face and body, to make herself nice to be near. When you indulge those around you in this way you're indulging yourself at the same time.

Of course I know that you're not going to go overboard. Establishing your nightly beauty routine doesn't mean that you're going to give up homework. It means that you like to look attractive and that you're beginning to appreciate yourself. Be glad that so many of the things that help you along the way are as nice to use as these beauty aids we are talking about.

And by "indulging yourself" I don't mean to say that you should do all of those delicious things that are actually bad for you. On the contrary. I want you to indulge yourself in those things that are *marvelous* for you, and for you to learn to enjoy doing them. Like warm, soaking tubs full of beautiful skin-softeners and oils instead of quick showers that only clean you. A bath can do so much more, not only for your body but for your head as well. Pamper yourself with foaming bath beads, or salts, or oils, all of which will help soften your skin, relax your nerves and please your other senses as well. Every great beauty in history, from Cleopatra to the ladies of the French court to the Hollywood stars, knew the luxury of sinking into a tubful of fragrant steaming water. And you have preparations available that those women never dreamed of, to encourage your taking care of yourself. Just be sure that you do not select those products that are heavily perfumed and thus full of drying alcohol. Read the printing on the packages carefully. It'll tell just what the ingredients of each product can do for you and whether there is anything that might be potentially unfavorable to your particular skin type. If you have any doubts, remember that the mildest, most natural preparations are the safest.

Remember too that the soothing bath water can help in a lot of ways. If you do your cleansing-toning-moisturizing just before you step into the tub, the warm water and air will help the moisturizer to penetrate even further into your skin. If you're putting ycur hair up dry or using an instant setter, the mist rising from the bath will help there too.

Even drying off afterward can be a plus, whether you prefer the invigorating briskness of a quick toweling off or the gentler patting dry of your body. Use a powder or a light spray cologne (perhaps in the same scent as your bath preparation, if you're really into luxury!) and you'll find you have turned the routine of the daily bath into a refreshing, relaxing beauty ritual.

Try to apply some of this "beautified thinking" to some of your other activities. You'll find yourself thinking and finding ways of building beauty habits that will last you forever and keep you forever looking good. Apply beauty ideas to things that you hate. Wouldn't doing the dishes be less distasteful if you knew that when you finished you were going to give yourself the benefit of a thorough hand-creaming? There is no area of the body other than the face that is so expressive, yet I find so many women neglecting their hands. Start to use hand lotion *now*, especially after your hands have been working or exposed to the outdoors, and you'll have hands that are a pleasure to touch and even to kiss. Women who have lovely well-groomed hands and know how to use them gracefully add another dimension to their charms, to their physical and personal beauty.

Now, here I must insert a word of caution. When I talk to you about the hands being well groomed, this is exactly what I mean: soft, smooth skin; clean, trim fingernails; pushed-back cuticles. What I *don't* mean is nail polish. I detest the look of nail polish on a young girl. Sometimes I still see children, little girls of five or six, with dark-red nails, and I think that there must be something terribly wrong with the mother who wants a child looking like that. Even for a girl in her teens I find polish very unnecessary. If you have used your hand cream regularly, filed your nails to a nice shape (and not three inches long like those of the Dragon Empress of China, which is certainly not a look for today's American girl) and trimmed your cuticles, and you still want to do something else, then perhaps a clear polish is a nice finish, although not strictly necessary. Care and grooming are what the hands need, not cosmetics.

Getting back to adding beauty to your thinking: picking up clothes and things from the floor may also be a bore, but think of it instead as a terrific stretching exercise for the back and legs and you'll start looking for reasons to bend down. It's great for the body.

These are just a few of the ideas you can rethink into part of your beauty routines. Knowing your own schedule, you can probably come up with many more. The important thing is to start thinking and doing those things that will enhance all of your assets. Make them so usual that after a while you'll do them without thinking about it. Then you'll find yourself doing beautiful things and becoming more beautiful as you do!

Makeup

Naturally, at this age one of the most important subjects is makeup. There is perhaps no other single thing you can use that announces so clearly to the rest of the world: "Look at me, I'm grown up." What I want you to be very concerned about and very conscious of is just *what* people will see when they do look at you—and your makeup.

Let's take the most important elements of makeup one by one. For the woman in her twenties and beyond, the most important item is, without question, *foundation*. But for those who have not yet reached that advanced stage of life, what is it?

Much as I insist upon foundation for almost every woman I make up, I feel differently about it where teenagers are concerned. Probably one woman out of a thousand *doesn't* need foundation; and I think that the reverse is probably equally true, that perhaps one young girl in a thousand *does*. Most teens who do use it do not understand what foundation can and cannot do.

It does not hide pimples and blemishes very well, though this is the purpose for which most girls use it. If you have discolorations on your face—if the skin is lighter or darker in some places than in others—a light foundation evenly applied will blend the various tones all together. But it's a general rule in makeup that anything you try to hide just becomes more noticeable. If you pour on gobs of foundation to hide your pimples, you will look as if you have poured on gobs of foundation to hide your pimples. You *won't* look as though you don't have pimples; you will only have made your problem more apparent.

Instead of trying to make makeup do what it can't, concentrate on making it do what it can—enhance your looks so that you look even better, *never* so that you look made up. This is a lesson for young and old alike, one that I never stop repeating. I am a makeup artist, yet I never want anyone to look at one of my clients and see her makeup. For me that is a defeat. It means I haven't done my work properly. When people look at one of my clients, I want them to see her looking better than she ever has looked before, but still see *her* and not the makeup.

That is exactly what I want you to achieve for yourself.

Let me tell you something: men, and especially young men, can be frightened by makeup. They don't want to see a lot of it on the women they like. Too much makeup, too much exaggeration on any woman says something about the woman the man does not want to hear. What a boy wants to see is you, looking as pretty and as natural as possible. If you suddenly appear in orange skin or a dark bronze in the middle of winter, in what way does that make you look better? And that is what makeup is all about—making you look better. But even better must be first of all believable or it won't be better at all.

I love the look of a rosy cheek, and if you don't have that naturally, I think that using some *rouge* is great. There are two different kinds that I like for young complexions, the cream rouge and the gel. Either one is easy to apply and gives a lovely, shiny glow to the cheeks.

Many girls like blush-on, which you apply with a brush, but I think that this sometimes looks a little powdery. If you really love it, use it only at night. How and where to apply your rouge is covered very thoroughly in the chapter on the cheeks.

As you may have guessed, I don't care for face powder on young complexions. Actually, this is a cosmetic I advise my older clients to use very sparingly, and I don't think young girls need it at all. With the money you save on not buying it, splurge on *lip gloss*. That's something I'm really in favor of!

Even if you are hesitant about using *any* makeup—and that's all right with me—lip gloss is a good idea. It can be your very first cosmetic. If ever a product was created with young looks in mind, gloss was definitely it. I prefer it to lipstick. Aside from being so pretty and so flattering on you, gloss has an *added* benefit. It's actually good for you to use. Every time you apply it you are giving your lips a moisturizing treatment that will help them to stay soft and smooth.

In addition to the clear gloss, you have a choice of many beautiful shades, almost as great a range as its older sister, lipstick. The choice is yours, but if you are extremely pale, or don't use any other makeup, then the lighter the shade of gloss, the prettier you'll look.

The next area for makeup is the *eyes*. Here we must proceed very cautiously. While I do believe that there is a lot a girl can do with eye makeup, the worry is always that she will do *too* much, which is worse than too little or none at all.

I think teenagers can use eye shadow with good results. The important thing to remember is that the look that you want is always crisp and fresh. You want to have a look of cleanliness about you, for the simple reason that this is the most appealing look a girl can have—and your appeal is what your makeup is all about. Exaggeration and vulgarity are out of place on any woman but especially on a teenager. The eye shadows to use are those of a neutral color rather than a glaring shade. The neutral color gives the eyes a very pretty look, making them look bigger and deeper without making you look made up. *The colors I recommend are taupe, very pale lavender and light brown*. Pick a shade that will flatter your eyes, and don't worry about matching the colors of what you're wearing, which is silly and unnecessary.

Mascara is nice to use too; I like the look of long, pretty lashes on a young face. But false eyelashes are absolutely o-u-t.

Don't use a thin, hard *liner* to outline your eyes. If you want to use any liner at all—which you really don't have to do—check the instructions in the eye-makeup chapter for achieving a soft, smudged look, which is simple and flattering.

If you wear *glasses*, use a little more mascara on your bottom lashes and try just a little bit of color under them. This should be applied with a pencil in a color that matches the shadow on your upper lid. Glasses tend to obscure the lower part of the eye, which is why you can use a little more there. Again, check the eye chapter for complete instructions.

Grooming for the eyes includes very careful *tweezing*. This is the right moment to start taking care of the strays, especially in the area between the two brows, above the bridge of the nose. Nothing can look sloppier than scraggly eyebrows, so start controlling them now. This doesn't mean going overboard and reshaping your brows completely, but following your natural arch and eliminating the few hairs that don't conform to it.

In talking about your eye makeup I must emphasize light, light, *light*. To use a little is pretty, to use too much is a disaster. It's up to you. And as I tell women of all ages, double-check your makeup in your mirror to see that it's all carefully applied.

Another area of beauty that you are ready to start exploring is that of *fragrance*. All of the bath beautifiers that you use may give you all of the scent that you want, and, indeed, it is a clean, fresh, pretty smell that clings to you after a bath. However, some girls might want a little more than that, and something that can be carried along during the day.

There are many lovely scents that you can buy in many different forms. I don't think you need the steepest-priced scent, which is perfume and which is the strongest form fragrance comes in. Cologne and toilet water, both available as sprays, should be sufficient. You can add to the scent you choose by using dusting powder, bath oils, body lotion and any other products that are made in the same fragrance. It's smart to use a scent this way, and it's very reassuring to know that your fragrance is as well coordinated as the clothes you wear.

As far as the fragrance itself is concerned, there are so many to choose from that would be suitable for you. I think that here your best bet is to consult the magazines that you look to for advice in other areas—*Seventeen, Glamour,* and *Mademoiselle*. These publications draw the advertisers who make the things that are usually meant for you. They will feature fragrances that are young in feeling, and young in price compared to the expensive perfumes that older women use and that really wouldn't be suitable for you at all. There are so many marvelous floral and outdoor, sporty scents being marketed now that it just doesn't make sense to spend more money than you have to for some grand important label. There's plenty of time later on to introduce yourself to that luxury.

I think of American girls as being clean, casual, bouncing with the kind of energy that in itself is good-looking and very attractive.

If there is one area where I must find fault, it is in the way most young girls today are wearing their hair. I'm talking about the long, long hair, hanging down the sides of the face, with all its oil and the dirt that the oil attracts, touching the cheeks and forehead and causing all sorts of problems besides that of general sloppiness.

Obviously I'm not talking about beautifully clean and expertly cut hair that is gloriously long and infinitely becoming to young—and only young—people. A marvelous mane of hair, if it's kept in top-notch condition, is one of the greatest assets and attractions a girl can have. But, unfortunately, most of the long hair I see is not kept this way. It seems to be just allowed to grow and do whatever it wants. It is parted in the middle, perhaps a comb is run through it once or twice, and then the owner forgets that it's even there. At least this is the way it looks. American girls, who do have the best hair in the world, are throwing away that fantastic advantage—one, by lack of proper care, and, two, by not wearing that glorious hair in the most becoming way possible.

I am not as expert in this area as any number of great and well known hairdressers are, many of whom have written their own books on the subject. What I am most concerned about is your hair as an important part of your over-all look—and believe me, you cannot achieve perfection with skin care and makeup if you ignore your hair.

Study yourself very carefully in the mirror. Is your hair really beautiful enough to justify having so much of it? If it is, fine. Just make sure it is washed often and kept shiny and smooth with the use of good conditioners. You might try just enough length to give it even more bounce and—very important—to keep it off your face.

If your hair is frankly not all that lovely, start thinking in terms of a new hair style. Again, one that has a lot of movement and bounce to it is marvelous, because hair is meant to have a lot of life to it, and hair that moves catches the light and looks lovely. If you want to wear your hair in the soft curly Afro that is so becoming to many girls, white and black, make sure that you use a good conditioner that will add both sheen and highlights. A smooth cap of close-cropped curls is a great look that is flattering to many different-shaped faces, and short hair is always easier to maintain than long.

I do think that hair, whatever the style, should be worn as much off the face as possible. Show your face, don't hide it behind masses of hair. Remember that hair, even dry hair, has a lot of oil in it, and when the oil of the hair touches the oil of the face, there is a disastrous collision. The explosion may be a rash or breaking-out of pimples and blemishes, because that great collection of oil is open house for infection to start.

The hair should be kept faultlessly clean of course, and I am in favor of very frequent washings. We bathe every day and nothing bad happens to our skin, and I'm not convinced that daily *shampooings*, with a mild soap, aren't equally beneficial for your hair. This country leads the world in manufacturing all sorts of hair conditioners, and I think you should use them frequently, picking the ones that are especially formulated for your hair. Other hair preparations, such as hair colorings, sprays, lacquers and the like, should be avoided. Your hair should look, smell and feel marvelous—which means clean and fresh, with nothing added to take away from its own naturalness.

The nasty effect of unclean hair falling on the face leads us to perhaps the most serious beauty problem of the teen years. Lucky is the girl who does not suffer to some degree or other from that unpleasant condition that haunts so many young people. I wish that there were something new I could tell you about how to avoid *acne*, but all I can do is tell you to pay attention to the suggestions I'm sure you've heard so many times. These include watching the foods you eat, being especially wary of those containing much oil or sugar. (The chapter on skin care will give you a good list of the foods that are beneficial to the skin.) Of course cleanliness is of the utmost importance, but if you are following the beauty steps I recommend for your skin type, then you are already doing yourself some good as far as combating the acne is concerned. Certainly keeping the hair off your face—as we were just discussing—is a step in the right direction. If we don't yet know how to prevent acne, at least we can do all of those things that we have found helpful in limiting it.

For the really extreme sufferer there are now surgical procedures available that can help heal the scars and perhaps remove the worst blemishes. For more information about this talk to your doctor or to a *dermatologist* in your area. If anyone can give you good advice about your skin, he can.

There is another, less serious, problem that affects many faces during the teens and that is the growth of unwanted *face hair*. This

condition can be more readily treated—best, I think, with the use of facial *wax*.

The thin, fine hair that suddenly starts to grow along the regular hairline *should be left strictly alone*. The only hair that I think should be waxed off—and only if there is a sufficient growth to be very noticeable—is the hair above the upper lip. I do not like the facial depilatories; I think the hair grows right back after these are used. The wax will remove the roots along with the hair, so one application might rid you of this problem for a good long time. If the hair is not really that conspicuous, don't bother.

Now we have treated both the pains and the pleasures of growing up female. In the field of beauty, happily, the goodies do outnumber the bad things, and I would like to see you take advantage of that fact. Do all the things that are good to do and are good for you. Learn those fine habits that you will keep for a lifetime. Exploring beauty when you're young has so many advantages besides that of getting a head start on good looks. For example, all of your friends are going through most of the same things that you are, so why not share experiences? Experiment with each other when you try new makeup and new hair styles. You can make a party of this sort of activity if you like.

Friends tend to be honest with each other, so you have a built-in audience to react to the changes you want to try on yourself. You can borrow products from each other, so that the allowance you get isn't blown on items you may be disappointed in. In addition to making beauty a pleasure—which it should be at any age—at your good time of life you can make it *fun* as well. There is a lifetime of beauty waiting for you, and the time to start is *now*.

CHAPTER TWELVE

As Years Go By

Most of the beautiful women I've met, consulted with, and have loved to spend my time with, have been over forty. I appreciate the maturity and sophistication that a woman of that age has acquired above the still rather unformed teenager.

Certainly the young girl has a physical loveliness that is at its height in those years. But when it comes to talking about life and fashion and travel and ideas, it is only the older woman who can have experienced and achieved the understanding that will be interesting to everyone.

I don't want to sound as though I don't enjoy young people; nothing could be further from the truth. But I must say what I feel, especially since it is in marked contrast to what I see and hear everywhere in this country. At fifty a woman in Europe is considered mature—yes, and also attractive and desirable. No one would call her old or over the hill—in fact, that expression exists only in America.

Most importantly, the European woman would never think of herself that way. A woman pays as much attention to herself at that age, as when she was younger, perhaps more. Her grooming is impeccable, her makeup perfection, her clothes so well put together as to create an aura of sophistication and luxe that can be acquired only with age. She has been experimenting for years, acquiring a sense of fashion, putting together a look that is truly her own style— something that every woman should be striving for if she hasn't yet achieved it. Your individuality is what makes you who you are. The mature woman who has this sense about herself has everything she needs to continue to be admired and wanted. This is within the reach of everyone, and it is something that lasts as long as life itself.

We must start with attitude changes. Again I look to Europe for my examples. There a model, for example, can still have an active career after she is well into her forties, and perhaps even longer. But in America the career of the fashion model is finished by the time she reaches twenty-five or thirty. European models who are no longer young continue to be very active because the European public appreciates the chic and refinement of maturing faces and the way they *add* so much to the clothes they endorse.

Of course we cannot expect all women to be blessed with such superlative, spectacular looks. But any maturing woman can learn a great deal from these celebrated women. You can learn the importance of being yourself, your best possible self, instead of retiring or, even worse, trying to imitate what you no longer are. Those are the two extremes that many mature women go to—too little or too much, too plain or too fancy. In between there are, I promise you, great ways to a loveliness you may have thought was past you. It is *not*.

When I talk to you about sophistication in grooming and fashion I do not mean either very extreme, severe looks or necessarily very expensive ones. What I mean is the kind of look that is at once a contrast to the carefree look of the youngsters and an emphasis on what is most becoming to you.

The mature woman on the Continent has a cultured look of refinement that we call *raffinée*. It can be very casual, but it is *not* throwaway casual. Let's be practical. The very young can perhaps afford to throw things away; the rest of us cannot. We are more *careful* of ourselves, our things, our time. Our look can be more studied, because we have had more time to study it. As babies we were like cubs or kittens, soft and cute and scruffy. As adults, looking scruffy no longer becomes us.

But I think that as one matures, the image, and even more important, the reality, that one wants to show is that of having accomplished something in life. For a man that probably means success. For a woman a better word is *chic*.

And true chic doesn't mean wearing a certain dress or acquiring a certain label. It literally starts at the fingertips and works its way over every fiber of your being. It is an attitude as well as a look, a state of mind as much as it is a closetful of clothes. One cannot look chic without first feeling chic—which is a result of striving very consciously for it.

As I have said, chicness starts at your very fingertips, and so shall we! I love the look of bright red polish on immaculately groomed hands. I realize that this will be considered by many people as being somewhat in the province of the young, but I don't agree. The cultivated look includes attention to all details of grooming, and next to the face, there is nothing more important than well-manicured hands. Many women as they age develop those brown spots, particularly on the backs of the hands, that are called age spots. If the hands are pale the spots will stand out. If the fingernails are a rich shade of red the spots will hardly be noticeable, the hands will look younger and well groomed.

Don't be afraid of bright colors. Used properly they can be your greatest aids. Maturing does not mean disappearing into the woodwork; it means making the most intelligent use of what you have.

Hair and hairdo are of vital importance to the mature woman. For almost everyone short hair is more flattering than long. A style that puts some fullness around the face, with simple soft lines, is good. It is preferred unless you have absolutely magnificent bone structure and high cheekbones like Katharine Hepburn's and your features would be enhanced by pulling the hair to the back of the head and letting everything on the face show.

And please let's talk about the flattery and good sense of gray and even white hair. Hair turns lighter by nature, and gray is a natural enhancer. Gray can be chic and elegant and very flattering, as light shades always are close to the face, whether it's pepper-and-salt at the temples or a streak of white on the crown or that fabulous effect that some women have naturally of the hair lightening at the hairline and deepening in color toward the back of the head. The important thing for gray hair is to keep it smashingly clean and well trimmed; and rinses should be added if necessary to keep it from looking yellowy.

Princess Stefanella Sciarra is one of the most important hostesses in Europe, and her hair is completely white. Countess Corti, her friend, is totally gray. They both look marvelous because their hair sparkles with light and highlights. Of course their grooming is always impeccable, and their vivaciousness is what really makes their parties such great events.

An American woman whom I greatly admire is Barbara ("Babe") Paley. She is one of the real American beauties, one of the chicest women anywhere she goes, and she just happens to have all the things I love most in a woman: her gray hair, her wonderful carriage, even the bump on her nose—all prerogatives of a mature woman. Were she to operate on her nose or dye her hair she certainly wouldn't improve that great individual look she has. I am willing to wager that the thought never occurred to her to do either. She breathes elegance and exudes chic.

It is hard for me to remember ever having suggested to a client that she dye her hair. I know that so many women do it, thinking that it makes them look younger, but usually the results show that one is making the effort but not succeeding.

Hair is never just one shade. Even the darkest black hair has many other shades and lights in it. Unfortunately, most hair colorists do not have the time or the understanding to reproduce what nature intended. They dye the whole head one color, making it look unnatural and unreal. Hair dyed black is usually even more obvious than a wig. As for colors—so many misguided women choose at a late stage in their lives to become improbable redheads. Better by far to have lovely, rich and believable gray hair that is properly cut and cared for.

With gray or white hair we want perfection in makeup. There are definite rules that apply to women with such hair coloring, which wouldn't work as well with darker shades. I love bright-red lipstick on gray-haired women for the same reason I recommend that they wear red nail enamel. As the skin ages it can grow paler or, in the case of black complexions, lose some of its tone. The bright reds and scarlets can really provide a lift to the face. While the pale pastels can be very pretty, I like the expressiveness of the bright colors better.

For a change from the bright red I like the flower shades. Light fuchsias, light pinks, such as petunia, and geranium colors. You can never go wrong if you choose the rose as a guide. Whether in a vase or on the mouth, the colors are always beautiful. Those are the shades that we in the cosmetics business borrow from nature. However, do not use orangey colors. With age the teeth tend to take on a yellowy cast, and orange will emphasize that. Very pale colors will not provide enough contrast to deaden the yellowing effect, so stick to those brighter shades.

Please be careful not to confuse *bright* with *dark*. The dark, maroony colors are disastrous on too pale or too ashy or sallow skins.

For the white- (and gray-) haired woman I also change the palette of eye-shadow shades. The neutral browns that I usually prefer are too muted for this coloring, but the blue shades I avoid spring to life. They work marvelously now. I don't like the bright aquamarine, sapphire or royal blues, but rather the subtle, murky colors with a touch of blue, such as slate, chinchilla, frosted grays, inky blues, the midnight shades. Just that touch of blue on the lids picks up and perks up the gray of the hair.

I don't like false eyelashes on an older woman, but prefer, instead, enormous amounts of mascara. A lot of mascara opens the eyes, livens the face and makes it young, giving that wide-eyed look brimming with life and curiosity about everything going on in the world.

Masks are marvelous for the skin and for stimulating the circulation—always important to promote healthy complexions. Especially at the age when skin becomes lax and loses tone, the mask becomes an important beauty aid. I'd like to see a mask used at least twice weekly, more often if possible. Make each application like a visit to a salon, right in your own bedroom. Apply a twenty- to thirty-minute mask, stretch out on the bed with pillows beneath your feet, cold compresses of eye lotion on your closed lids, eight-hour cream on your hands and lips. Turn the phone off and do nothing for that half hour. Doze if you can, and wake up feeling refreshed and divine, ready to take on the world. You will be! You have just given your skin, and yourself, a little mini-vacation that will reap marvelous dividends. There are many such masks being sold at cosmetic counters.

Or you can get a firming-lifting treatment by using a mask *every day* for one week each month. It's like going to Switzerland or Aspen for the week. The skin responds to this kind of concentrated effort almost as if it were a so *simpatico* shock treatment.

Now that the skin has been properly stimulated, it is ready for the routine skin-care steps, and then on to the foundation. Here too a change in color may be in order. A touch of *peach* or *pink* in the foundation will help the over-all coloring.

Many women make the mistake of using heavier rather than *lighter* foundation as they grow older. Heavy foundations will not cover up flaws or lines. In fact, the effect is exactly the opposite. In half an hour or an hour heavy foundation will crack, seep into the lines you thought it would hide, and end up exaggerating them instead, emphasizing what you tried to conceal. An older woman should select a foundation that is light, creamy and moisturizing, preferably made with a water base. Application should always be with a sponge, which is best, especially for the thinner compounds.

Never, never let anyone see you without your *rouge* on: that should be a cardinal rule. It make the difference between looking good and . . . not looking good. Whether you select cream rouge or the brush-on type, every morning should start with a cold-water face rinse, application of moisturizer, and if nothing else until later, a dab of rouge on the cheeks. An immediate, 100 percent improvement—and who doesn't need that in the morning?

The rouge color should always be bright, such as burgundy or other winy shades. Brown is forbidden, so is coral, which turns to yellow, as does orange. Remember that rouge is instant health so far as your looks are concerned, and should be applied as regularly as medicine. Its far nicer, though, and the results are immediately visible.

The colors that you *wear* are as important as those you put on your face. The colors I love on maturing women are *soft*, with one important exception—that bright lacquer *red* again, certainly smashing on an older woman. Red is a happy color. If you don't think it's for you, try it on and then try on something in brown, just to see the difference.

A classic color and the color of so many classic clothes is *navy blue*. Trimmed with touches of white or worn with lots of gold jewelry, it is always in good taste and knows no season.

White, once considered a summer color only, is marvelous even in winter. A white suit or a dress with a black blazer will take you anywhere in the world.

Gray, that pale, pearly, dove gray, is terrific. It lets you be the protagonist—you are wearing your clothes, and they're not wearing you. Gray flannel in a marvelous pant suit, or a lovely cotton pin-stripe—really, the possibilities are endless.

All the good shades of *beige* are in order. Avoid the drabs with yellowish casts to them. But the straws, the honeys, the wheats, even the pale, pale eggshells are very chic colors. Beige that goes into peach is fine too. Rose beige and tea rose are great flatterers.

Peach itself is a good color for you—again, if it doesn't have a yellow or apricot cast. It should be a warm, cosmetic, appealing peach.

Pink is almost always right. Schiaparelli's famous Shocking Pink and the beautiful—I must admit—pink of Elizabeth Arden that we call Arden Pink are totally flattering to a woman. The baby pinks, the powders, the pales, the brights—wear them all.

There are stupendously chic shades in winter colors that are good for you: *rust* or *russet* is marvelous but needs careful accessorizing; *burgundy*, not purple but with a touch of gray in it—a deep, deep color; *forest* or *cypress* green, best with a softer color close to the face—a shirt or scarf—to make the green really work for you.

Black is good, but it has complications. It is serious, maybe too somber. Black needs to be well accessorized, to have something to cut it, to interrupt the black: lots of gold, touches of color or white. Black, when it's formal, demands diamonds or pearls. No rhine-stones, no sequins, no pretense. Black for day can be terrific. What a stunning look this is: a white-haired woman in black turtleneck sweater and slim pants, with a red pea jacket! I'm sure you can come up with many variations on that theme.

Stay away from loud prints, large patterns, overbold, optical-illu-sion geometrics. There is nothing attractive there. They do not add style but present the problem of how on earth to accessorize them. Large florals are all right for your mattress or the tea towels in your kitchen, but please, not *on* you.

Much new fashion is for the very young, for those who have not yet found themselves and so are ready to try anything that comes along, no matter how ridiculous. And I do mean ridiculous. You can take almost any of last year's styles and look at it today to see what I mean. When was the last time you saw someone in a mini-skirt? And when you did, didn't she look all wrong? In their time they seemed destined to last forever, but now they're practically forgotten.

Only the classics go on eternally, and the classics are great for any age, and certainly for the mature. By classic I mean well-cut pants and blazers, suits modeled after the famous Coco Chanel's, the clean-cut look that is always identified with the best in American sportswear. The woman who chooses classic, whether it's the undying camel's-hair coat or the tailored shirt, always looks as if she knows exactly what she's doing. And she has another great advantage: the simplicity of classic clothes makes them perfect for accessorizing, and that's where her developed fashion sense comes in.

Instead of investing heavy amounts of money in looks that could easily be outmoded by the time they're paid for, the truly chic woman buys fashion in bits and pieces—in other words, accessories. Scarves, jewelry, belts, sunglasses (which I really love as a terrific fashion prop), all can mirror your awareness of what is current and chic without your having to give up your own style and give in to what may be totally wrong for you.

The classic looks should also embody those features that are most relevant to the *needs* of the maturing woman. You *need* sleeves, because the upper arms are the first part of the body to show age—and the surest way of showing age is by trying to dress young. A suggestion of nudity on the part of a mature woman would be ghastly. Deep décolletage, bare backs, hip-high slits are not for you. While they might look smashing on the young, they are demeaning and undignified on older women. Remember that chic encompasses dignity, and that all the most civilized ancient peoples covered their women very modestly. Many still do.

This brings me to another fashion. While it could hardly be called an American classic, it is showing all the signs of becoming a mainstay of many of our smartly dressed women. This is the *caftan*. The style we see most frequently originated in Morocco, and it's a natural for the older woman, whether she is as thin as Gloria Guinness or as well endowed as TV's Maude. One can't go to work in a caftan, but for entertaining at home, dining out or at resorts it's unbeatable. A caftan is almost as flexible as a dress, in that it can be as simple or as formal as you want. The lines, the shape of the garment is where the enormously feminine flattery lies. While every age group has adopted them, to the older woman they are a godsend. In a caftan one is well covered but still very soft, very feminine-looking, with a hint of mystery that is attractive to men. I love the flow of the caftan as well as the great range of fabrics and styles.

Even though the caftan and certain other fashions tend to conceal the figure, I don't want you hiding anything—by that I mean excess weight. We do need less rather than more food as we grow older, and it is a good kind of sacrifice to make—less eating for less poundage. I can think of almost no one who is overweight and chic. An elegant slimness is the body condition that every woman should be striving for, and there are diet plans that insure safe weight loss with maintenance of health. The Duchess of Windsor, already in her middle years when Edward VII married her, was never really a raving beauty. But she had a lot going for her. She had a sense of herself that she never deviated from. Even if you have no plans to topple a government, there is a lot to be learned from her.

Although she spent a lot more money on clothes than most women are able to afford, she kept her wardrobe simple and wore her clothes for years. She had a look that she kept forever. Her whole concept was very interesting and she's stuck to it all her life. The same hairdo—parted in the middle, close to the head, caught up in a chignon at the nape of the neck. The same clothes style— everything very tailored, mostly suits, about which she said, "My wardrobe is very simple, each year the same colors in different styles." Though all these principles might not apply to your life style, here is a great deal of food for thought.

I don't mean that everyone should pattern herself on the Duchess of Windsor. Her style was right for her physically, as yours must be for you. But finding *your* pattern, *your* point of view, and sticking to it because it's right for you, is the great lesson we can all learn from her.

In order to develop a fashion point of view, you should realize what you feel good in and know that you look better in some things than others. Concentrate on that until you have the backbone of your wardrobe. Perfect the look with excellent tailoring, impeccable grooming and your individual looks; you're using the good sense and knowhow that only experience can bring. You're taking advantage of what you've been brainwashed to think is a disadvantage. The individuality that you develop now can carry you with grace through the next twenty or thirty or however many years. The beautifully finished polished look takes great pains and discipline to achieve, but it's worth it because you can keep it yours forever.

Another important aspect of your body, now that you are on your way to perfecting *you*, is the posture with which you carry it. You should always hold yourself erect, whether sitting or standing. There is nothing so aging, in appearance and actually, as a slumped-down, slouched body. The head should be held high, the shoulders back, the stomach tucked in. A young girl may be a princess, but a mature woman should have the carriage of a queen.

Now you will want to take a good look at your *surroundings* and see if they exemplify you and help to enhance you. A good way to begin to make your home help you is to *dim* the lights. This is what every intelligent older European woman does when she entertains. If the occasion calls for it, turn the lights out completely and depend totally on candlelight, which is about the most marvelous thing you can do for yourself.

Next best to candles is the light that is achieved by using pink bulbs in lamps with shades of natural raw silk, which are pale beige in color and of a shantunglike texture. This combination puts a most beautiful glow on everyone's face, for which your guests will be everlastingly grateful to you.

The colors of the rooms in which you live should be carefully thought out. So should the *textures*. I prefer to see a room decorated in the cheapest kind of cotton—that marvelous mattress ticking, for instance—rather than draped in pompous velvets. The ticking, only one example, is imaginative, a fresh idea, especially when you consider the effect of funereal drapes of fake brocade or old museum velvet. Life is no longer lived with formality amidst Victorian leftovers. Your home should honestly reflect you and your modern life style.

That doesn't mean you can't indulge in flights of fancy. Some of the best effects are borrowed from faraway places, yet suit our ways superbly. I'm thinking of the sun-drenched all-white rooms in the Mediterranean and Caribbean villas I've seen. Merle Oberon in her house in Mexico has an all-white room; you have to be barefoot to enter. Everything, from the carpeted floors to the ceiling, is white. The only touch of color is very pale beige—little wicker baskets here and there. The effect is that of total serenity and total calm, which reflects on the faces of all who are inside it. There is nothing to hurt the eyes, so there is nothing to cause a frown. You must feel beautiful in a room like that.

A certain room in a house on the other side of the world is done in deep tones, with peach walls and furniture, the only other colors being supplied by tables lacquered in plum and the brown floor. This combination throws a cosmetic glow on the faces of the occupants.

An ultramodern apartment in Milan is a perfect reflection of its owner. Deep burgundy carpeting, stainless-steel accents and *gray flannel walls* make a background for a woman with short, curly, gray hair, who knows exactly how best to set herself off in her home.

Pauline Trigère, one of the greatest American women designers, loves red as dearly as I do, and, to prove it, has a room covered in nothing but. Another woman of infinite taste, Diana Vreeland, has red-lacquered walls and carpeting printed to look like fur. Scented candles are always burning to keep the senses stimulated. Your fragrance, too, should surround you like a trademark, your signature, which makes an unforgettable impression.

I have cited these examples like candles to stimulate you and set you thinking. Think of the ambiance in which you are going to be seen by those who come to your home. On entering your living room, people will see the surroundings first, then they will see you as an entire being. This is the first impression you make and the reason that it is so important to have a sense of *proportion* about yourself. People should see *you*, not a hairdo that overpowers everything else or a dress that shouts to be seen, drowning out the person who is actually wearing it. They should see your rooms as surroundings that express *you*.

I don't mean to suggest that this is the only reason that your interiors are important. Primarily, your home should give *you* a sense of well-being, a feeling of comfort in knowing that here is a place that truly reflects you and everything you have accomplished in life. Your home, whether it is an apartment, a house, a mansion or a castle, should be a center of serenity, brimming with what you love. No matter how much one travels—and I hope that traveling is an important part of everyone's life—there is a certain sweetness in

coming home that is one of the happier emotions in life, or should be. See that it is in yours. Aside from your own physical presence, there is nothing that is such a measure and reflection of you as your home. Especially as the years go on, we come to appreciate the center of gravity and respository of memories that home comes to mean. To enjoy it to its utmost, cultivate and care for it as you do for yourself.

I am a great believer in luxury. To me true luxe is the best of good taste. Coco Chanel said, "Some people think luxury is the opposite of poverty. It is not. It's the opposite of vulgarity." I think everybody deserves as much luxury as he or she can afford; the longer we live, the more we are entitled to! *Be good to yourself to the greatest degree you can afford to be—there lies happiness!* I don't care if it's giving yourself a sumptuous sable coat or a sumptuous thirty-minute facial, it all adds up to the same thing, taking care of yourself. By all means, be your own best friend. In turn, that makes other people want to be your friends too.

Remember that your best, as the poet Robert Browning put it, is yet to be. Strive for and achieve that best every day.

CHAPTER THIRTEEN

Considering Cosmetic Surgery

Almost every woman has fantasized about what cosmetic surgery can do for her. A great number of women look into that silvery glass and do not like what they see. Even extremely attractive women want to make changes in themselves. One is unhappy with her nose. Another is worried about the sagging of her eyelids, while her best friend is concerned about the bags under her eyes. Yet another decides that her eyes themselves are the problem—they are too small and need a face-lift to make them look larger. Or someone's cheeks are collapsing or ears are protruding or . . . or . . . or . . .

What fascinates me is that American women, so strong in their pursuit of careers, so keen in their sense of fashion, so eager to receive the most avant-garde ideas, are still so vulnerable and insecure about their beauty. They don't realize that one's own look, one's own individuality is the greatest thing going for a woman. To change or conceal or operate on this wonderful uniqueness is a terrible waste. You should see the specialness that is you and enhance, not destroy it.

The perfect oval face we used to think of as the ideal is really a mixed blessing. It will age more rapidly than faces with less regular features, which will grow more interesting with years. Perfect, symmetrical beauty will fade, while more irregular features become distinctive and characterful.

Look at those who are considered the outstanding women of our day; they are no longer the glamor girls of the twenties and thirties. In fact, even twenty years ago they wouldn't have been considered of movie-star caliber. Times and our concept of true beauty have changed; we should all take advantage of it.

Barbra Streisand was one of the first to reverse the trend toward conformity with her famous refusal to straighten her nose. And how right she was! When you look at her you see a fabulous creature whose eyes, whose hands, whose style enchant. Her special, beautiful features helped make her the only female star with *guaranteed* box-office success.

Charlotte Rampling is another girl who would never have made the grade in Hollywood's heyday. Yet her unique, off-balance features fill the screen with more excitement than do those of almost any other actress.

Liza Minnelli, whose enormous eyes dominate, is a most dynamic personality. She too knows how to make her features work.

The most interesting women in the world today are those who are completely themselves. They are originals, having realized that it is better to be unique than to be anyone's copy.

Remember that whether or not you like every one of your features, they all combine to work together for a total look. One cannot correct one feature without considering all of the others carefully. You shouldn't ask for Grace Kelly's nose if it would leave your chin looking as if it belonged to Gene Kelly.

This is a matter of balance, easily understood with the help of a coffee cup, a saucer and a dinner plate. Put the cup on the saucer and both on the plate. See the perfect symmetry of the three. The proportions are perfect. But suppose you think that the saucer is too large (and let's pretend the saucer is your nose). You remove it, leaving the coffee cup in the center of the dinner plate. See what happens: you become strangely aware of the size and width of the dinner-plate area when the object of smaller proportions is sitting in its center. Now put back the saucer. Everything falls into place again.

Many women look at themselves and see the ideal reshaping, but not in the necessary context of the face. Often the decision to have cosmetic surgery is an emotional one rather than one based on a carefully thought-out recommendation from a doctor. And because cosmetic surgery seems to work miracles, many women look to it as a cure-all for problems, beauty and otherwise. But does it really work the miracles you want?

Is there an older woman alive who has never stood in front of her mirror and pulled her skin back with her fingers to see what a face-lift could do for her? What mature woman doesn't stretch the skin back and try to look younger? But this approach is wrong in many ways.

In the first place, you stretch your skin back with your fingers right on your face! No surgery could possibly be done at the places your fingers are positioned; you'd have scars all over your face. The surgery is done behind the hairline, where scarring won't ever show, much further back from where your fingers are. And of course the farther you go from the area, the less pull is achieved. Looking at a face-lift this way is unrealistic, to say the least.

Another mistake many women make in facing the mirror is in their *approach*. They search for the bad points instead of the good ones on their own faces. That goes back to what I was saying about being so vulnerable about one's looks. I think it's very important to confront your mirror without any negative feelings. You should approach the glass with love, optimism and a bit of humor. Don't take yourself too seriously. Savor yourself as you should everything else in your life—with a grain of salt.

Your attitude becomes a part of your makeup in the most tangible way. Putting on makeup and thinking that it's going to make you look good will make you look good and feel good. Your happy attitude will be reflected in your eyes, in the upturn of your mouth, where only your attitude can reach.

A negative attitude will not give you a true evaluation of how you look to others. When others look at you they do not scrutinize your face for faults. They see the best things, points they like and admire and even envy. To really see yourself as others see you, look at and concentrate on your good points.

All of my ideas on makeup and beauty are based on solidly proven principles that I've put into use thousands of times. I've seen just how well these simple rules work. And I never underestimate the importance of the positive frame of mind behind the face.

I think of surgery only as a last resort, for only the most extreme cases. I seldom recommend it to a client. Progress and techniques in this surgery come from work done on women—and men—who have had facial damage as the result of an accident; this is what it is truly meant for. For the average woman, who merely wants to improve her appearance, I have developed a series of makeup routines that can take the place of surgery, providing almost as beneficial results.

Frankly I find this approach much healthier than undergoing cosmetic surgery. As I have said, learning to live with—and perhaps agreeing to enhance—your flaws is a free and liberating exercise in individuality.

Making Up Instead of Making Over

AREA: THE CHIN

Because chin implants have become routine, many women with weak or receding chins want to have this silicone-implant operation. But is it really necessary? The lower part of the face is not the more prominent; you already know that I don't believe the mouth should dominate the face. If you are unhappy with your chin, you can very easily remedy the situation, not with expensive surgery, but merely by concentrating all of your fashion makeup on the upper part of the face—where it should be anyway!

By this I mean using more makeup on your *eyes*. Experiment with those shades of eye shadow recommended for your individual coloring. Try using *more* color than you ordinarily would. Increase the amount of mascara—something you can almost never get too much of. Use greater amounts of neutral colors that create depth and intensity about the eyes and make them magnetic and irresistible.

A greater amount of *rouge*, carefully applied and blended toward the eyes and temples, will create more interest in the upper face and draw more attention to it. Eye and cheek makeup should be predominant on *any* face as this is the area of most visual contact, and will certainly serve to neutralize the area you least want noticed.

AREA: THE EYES

Sagging under the eyes is a very common problem. This is due to the fact that there are no oil glands located there. The skin tends to become very dry and transparent. Here help becomes a matter of *application*.

Long false eyelashes drooping over the trouble spot aren't going to work. What is needed is a very careful application of the right colors. Light colors will look wrong because they emphasize the crepiness and puffiness of the skin. The desired effect here is a *deepening* of the eyes, to detract from the circles below, which is accomplished through the use of dark colors on the upper lid and lots and lots of mascara.

The puffiness can also be further camouflaged by the use of a *concealing cream. Dark circles under the eyes* will be hidden by concealing cream and minimized by using a *darker shade of rouge* around the entire cheek area.

Many women of all ages would like to have bigger eyes, or at least give the illusion of them. It certainly doesn't pay to undertake the surgery that opens the eyes by pulling up the brow unless you have a great many lines in that area that you also want to get rid of. But there is much that *makeup* can do for enhancing and opening the eyes without your having to go to extremes of any kind in order to achieve the desired look.

If you feel your eyes are *set too close* together, use a light shade of eye shadow, starting from the inner corners and going to midway on the lower part of the lid, blending into a darker shade on the outer portion. Then apply a little of the darker color past the outer corner, going toward the temples, blending carefully with your foundation so that there is no line of demarcation. When putting on mascara, use the same principle, varying only the amount, not the color. Apply most of the mascara on the outer lashes, making a thicker application than you do on the inner lashes. Again, this has the effect of widening the eyes and drawing attention to the outer area. Check your brows; see that they are widely spaced, each starting directly above the inner corner of the eye, *not* somewhere over the bridge of the nose. Nothing does more to make eyes look closely set than brows growing inward toward each other. Clearing the area between the brows can be done easily with your tweezers. Use your tweezers too for keeping brows thin and naturally formed. The less brow, the more open-looking the eye will be.

Even the *small eye* can be made to look more open and thus larger. Put additional emphasis on the lower lashes. Be sure to use mascara on them and a touch of color beneath them. This should be in the same shade as the shadow on the upper lid, applied in a soft line from the center of the lashes to the outer corners. Always apply a greater amount of any eye makeup from the midway point to the outer corners. The upper part of the top lids should be shadowed in a color such as light brown, which will make it *recede*. Never use highlighter or shades such as pink or yellow here. They will serve to emphasize the bone, which you want to make less obtrusive. *Never use white* eye shadow at all, for the same reason. If you want to add false eyelashes, they must not be applied as a strip for the whole lash area. Rather, apply single lashes *only* at the outer corners. This is a bit difficult to master but can have a very beautiful effect on small eyes.

What we are doing here is using a little common sense by applying the principle of balance to the face. The amount of makeup, the colors, the careful application serve to outweigh the problem area and thus minimize it. Without surgery.

Remember this principle as well: the older one gets, the more these problems seem to increase. Surgery at the first sign of a line or a wrinkle may be futile, as time is only going to bring the problem back. Clever use of makeup is like fighting a holding action, keeping you looking good without your having to resort to the extreme of surgery until and unless it becomes an imperative. And in most cases it simply will not become one.

AREA: THE FACE

There is nothing more helpful than hair when you're trying to change the look of the size or shape of your face. Hair has volume and can do more to correct facial flaws than makeup itself. That is quite an admission for a makeup artist to make, but it is the truth. Though I am not a hair stylist, I very often suggest types of hair styles to my clients.

If the face is a work of art, the hair style is the frame. Because there is such a closeness between the two, the hair helps determine the shape and the look of the face.

I like shorter hair on an older woman. Not the extreme, short, geometrical cut that simply shears away all the beauty of the hair but the kind of short style that has volume, sweeps up from the face and provides some fullness about it.

Shorter hair gives you a nicer back and longer neck—a longer silhouette in fact, which gives a younger, lighter look. I don't believe in a lot of fussy curls and ringlets à la the Empress Eugénie, but there should be some fullness to the crown and some softness around the face.

What must be avoided at all costs is the younger-generation look of long hair parted in the middle, hanging down the sides. The way to look younger is *not* to adopt the hair style of your daughter, because then you merely look as though you are in competition with her—and losing.

You might want to consider hair coloring. If you do, I would suggest not an over-all color change, which seldom works the way you want it to, but a *lightening* of the hair closest to the face, blending into your regular color in a natural, believable way. This is highly flattering.

All of these measures serve to give a lift to the face and its contours. But the right hairdo can even help certain features. A large nose, for example, can be helped into better proportion by giving more volume to the hair and thus creating the illusion of a larger head. It's the plate and the cup and saucer again, the idea of balance and proportion.

A hairdo can help a too-round face as well. There is no surgery that can change a full cheek to a flat cheek. If you're born with marvelous high, hollow cheekbones—wonderful; but if not, forget it. Disguise some of the fullness with a smart pageboy or a style that ends in a little *guiche* on the cheek. As long as the curl is bouncy against the face, not lacquered down, it's a very pretty look.

You can also counteract fuller cheeks by using one of my very favorite fashion accessories, something that gets smarter all the time, tremendous sunglasses. They're so chic, I love them. Barbara Walters, Jackie Onassis and Sophia Loren all get great mileage out of their enormous glasses. Barbara Walters wears almost clear lenses on TV so that you can see her eyes, Jackie O prefers the dark glasses that give her a degree of privacy, and Sophia uses hers to emphasize her beautiful eyes. A very large frame will do wonders for a round face. It's a marvelous *today* look, as attractive on older women as it is on younger ones. With these you can give yourself a touch of fashion, a touch of youth, an aid to your contouring, knowing that it is entirely appropriate and in great taste.

Of absolutely no help is the old trick of trying to hide full cheeks by means of cosmetic shading. It simply doesn't work. It's fine for a model who is professionally acquainted with her face and can color and shade it for the best camera and lighting advantages. But it won't do in real life. You cannot control the lights you're under or the angle at which people will look at you, nor can you remain in one position without moving your head. And every time any one of these three ordinary factors shifts just slightly, all of the shading you may have done is seen for just what it is—stripes of color on your face. I don't give any instructions for such application in this book, and if you should find it elsewhere, my advice is to ignore it. It has nothing to do with the real world. *Anything that shows what you've tried to do doubly defeats its own purpose. Rouge,* blended toward the temple, will help sculpt a flat cheek with interest and create a cheekbone.

AREA: THE NOSE

We have talked about how helpful a hairdo can be in bringing a large nose into better proportion. I should like to add to that much the same advice that I gave in regard to deemphasizing a weak chin: play up the eye and cheek makeup. Careful application of foundation so that there is no undue attention brought to it, the use of face powder in small amounts to keep it from getting shiny and conspicuous—both work well. Again, no special shading of foundation colors—one sneeze and you'll look like a finger painting.

I happen to like aquiline noses. Romans consider them a sure sign of aristocracy. Every Roman princess has a bump on her nose to go with her *palazzo*. Both are part of the inheritance, and an aquiline nose is never considered to be a flaw on a face. Also, there is nothing with which one can embellish a nose—a sign that it was meant to be left alone. A nose can grow with age, not only in size but, more important, in character. A large nose on an older person is not so startling. It is quite in keeping with the signs of life that time has etched on the face, characteristics of having lived and loved which I for one would never dream of erasing. Everything that happens to the face is part of the sum total of what we are. Taken with a good measure of self-esteem, we can and should love the result.

Makeup After Surgery

I must admit to the possibility that there is someone whom I have not convinced to forgo surgery. And there is also the likelihood that many readers have already had various procedures done. For those who want to investigate the possibilities it is a relatively simple matter. Your own physician can recommend a skilled cosmetic surgeon to you, or the county medical society can supply you with a list of all the practitioners in your area. It's not difficult to locate a very skillful, reputable cosmetic surgeon close to home, or in a large city farther away if you want to keep the matter quite secret.

After surgery the problem becomes a different one: what do you do about your makeup *now?*

For the past several years I have worked very closely with some of the leading cosmetic surgeons and their patients on this very question. Too many women, having decided that they absolutely must have corrective surgery in order to enhance their looks, *then go back to the same makeup they always used*, considerably reducing whatever effect the doctors have accomplished for them.

This can be a disaster, because usually the woman who is that troubled about her wrinkles or her nose has gotten into the habit of using very heavy makeup in order to conceal the problem. This of course didn't work before the surgery, and it certainly isn't going to do any good after it.

You should not use any makeup whatsoever *immediately* after the surgery. You have to wait until the doctor tells you it's all right. And I can tell you that it will be several weeks after surgery before you can really admire your new self. It's only in the movies that the doctor lifts the bandage from the star's face, and there she is—immediate perfection, every eyelash in place.

The reality, I'm afraid, is far less lovely. You come out of the operation with discoloration, puffiness, stitches, bruises, dried blood in your hairline where the scars are—more like the victim of a car crash than the divine new self you were expecting. These effects last only for a short time, but during that time you will be feeling very sorry for yourself, and perhaps regretting having taken such a step. And once your doctor tells you that you can start wearing makeup again, your first job will be to hide all those signs of healing. For this you will want concealing cream and foundation in a heavier formulation than I usually prefer, such as a stick or thick cream, but just for a short while.

The concealing cream should be applied softly and carefully with a *brush*. Remember, you have rather recent incisions and sutures which you don't want to be stretching. That's why the brush is best for this application. Then *sponge* on your foundation for as much coverage as you can get. If you have selected a stick foundation, don't use it as an applicator. The sponge is gentler and pats on more easily, with less pull on your face than the repeated strokes the stick requires. Use little or no face powder, perhaps only on the nose. Powder will show up any caking of the extra foundation. Just content yourself with an enormous amount of foundation to even out all the discolorations and other problems until they disappear.

If you have had an incision in the middle of the eyelid don't use anything there, but do put some color on the very lowest part of the lid, just above the lashes, and just a bit of brown below the brow. A touch of color, with pencil, beneath the bottom lashes always looks pretty. Use small amounts of all of these cosmetics so that *removal* will be easy with a cotton swab and you won't have to do a great deal of rubbing. You need to be very careful.

The period following a face-lift or eye operation, or indeed any cosmetic surgery, is an ideal time to consider a great new pair of frames for your regular glasses or for sunglasses. Choose a frame different from the style you've been used to—a bigger frame, tinted lenses, a great new look. This is not the time to have your face totally exposed, shouting to the world that you've had something done to it. It will take you time to get used to the new face; it will take other people some time as well. The big glasses are good camouflage, good therapy, good fashion too!

If you undergo a face-peel or dermabrasion or any of the chemotherapy *procedures for renewing the skin*, the first makeup you use afterward must involve a totally different approach. If the skin is new and somewhat *raw*, you want the lightest possible foundation and rouge. Use water-soluble foundations that can rinse off easily. Avoid gels; they may stain the new skin. Use sponges or brushes to apply everything; they are kinder to the skin than fingers or anything else. Sponges provide the skin with less penetration by pigments and other ingredients; brushes don't pull at the skin. Sponge on foundation (always my preferred application at any time), sponge on cream rouge, or brush on dry-brusher. Use all of the skin makeups lightly; concentrate on your eyes.

But with all of these precautions in mind, *and only after your doctor's go-ahead*, do adopt a makeup routine. Makeup is a marvelous tonic for anyone, especially for you at these moments when you may be feeling very unsure of yourself because you're facing the immediate aftermath of the operation and not the final results.

And once your new face has settled itself, it is time to rethink your makeup. The waiting time may be just one week for a nose procedure, two weeks for an eye correction, and as long as three or four weeks after a total face-lift. If you ever read a magazine story in which a woman tells about having a face-lift on Friday and dinner for twelve on Monday, don't believe it. Modern procedures can seem rather miraculous in this area; but they are still very far from being overnight affairs.

Much more constructive is what you should do to maintain and enhance your new-found face. Your moisturizer is more important than ever. Use it faithfully. Use beauty masks, lubricating creams, and any other skin conditioners that your doctor recommends, because all of these will help the skin look supple and younger longer.

Use your own most gentle and intelligent *touch* on your face. Never stretch the skin—ever. Pat, stroke, touch. Even with the new makeup that you will use after the waiting period is over, stay with your sponges and brushes.

About that makeup. You took ten years off your face—now do the same with your makeup! First, forget about all the heavier consistencies, darker colors and other things you were using to hide the so-called flaw that has now been corrected. Dark lipstick, the pancake makeup—such things are deadly and aging. They should never be resorted to in the first place and should certainly be discarded now!

If you've lifted your face, what you want to do now is *lighten your makeup*. Actually, all of the same rules apply here that I gave for the woman who wants to look younger or more attractive without surgery. A *light*, *soft* hairdo, a *bright* rather than dark lipstick, a perky, *healthy* cream rouge.

If you need to lose weight, do it *before*, not after, a face-lift. A new hairdo, new grooming, new clothes will alone account for much of the change in you. All this validates your looking different.

The makeup procedures that I have detailed in all the chapters in this book will give you an improved appearance radical enough to hide the fact of your surgery. You can give Pablo's book all the credit and keep your surgery your secret! Unfortunately, cosmetic surgery has become a status thing to brag about—like a yacht or a Picasso in the bathroom. And that is one of the reasons that so many women are having it done so unnecessarily, to my thinking.

Which brings me full circle to where we started: my strong feeling that, in the first place, your flaws can make you fascinating, and in the second, they can be minimized with intelligent use of makeup. I still stand by these beliefs and would dearly love to challenge anyone on them!

CHAPTER FOURTEEN

Pablo's Most Frequently Asked Questions

Q. Why don't my rouge and blushers stay on?

A. Probably because you have an oily skin, and in that case you must make sure that you use a mild *astringent* before you put makeup on. The combination of rouge (cream rouge preferably) over foundation, a light powder if necessary, *and* dry blusher over the powder will insure a longer-lasting blush.

Q. My makeup runs easily. How can I make it stay on longer?

A. Make sure that you use a mild astringent, which will correct the acidity of your skin, and limit the amount of moisturizer you use. Frequent blotting with tissue after cleansing, after refreshing, after moisturizing and after foundation will insure a longer-lasting makeup.

Q. Do I need a moisturizer even though my skin is oily?

A. Yes. You should never confuse oil with water; even the oiliest skin needs water. You should limit the amount of moisturizer and use *practically none* of it on areas such as the forehead, nose and chin, which have more oil glands than elsewhere.

Q. How can I prevent my eye shadow from creasing?

A. By avoiding cream or paste eye shadows and using cake or pressed-powder eye shadows instead. Also, make sure that the area of the lid is completely or almost completely grease-free. If you have applied some moisturizer there, blot it. If you use foundation on your lid, blot that as well, then apply the eye shadow and buff it with the applicator.

Q. What can I do so my mascara will not smudge below my eyes and make me look as if I have dark circles?

A. Make sure that the skin in the area underneath the eyes is not too oily. While you don't want to powder that area too much, because you will get a dry, wrinkled, crepey look, a mild blotting with a tissue and the lightest brush-powder application may be desirable. Make sure that your mascara is completely dry before you close your eyes or the mascara will smudge. If your lashes are long and straight, and if you look down and blink frequently during the day, your lashes will touch the skin and leave mascara on it. There are certain mascaras that are waterproof and some that are oil-proof. When a mascara is not oil-proof it mixes with the oils on your skin and thus tends to smudge. If you carry a sponge with you, such as the one that you apply your foundation with, you can easily wipe the smudge out, blot and then powder lightly.

Q. Why do I have more lines around the eyes than on the rest of my face?

A. Because the eye area is completely without oil glands, therefore it is the one that ages first. Also, by smiling and talking and making facial expressions we raise our cheekbones and the area around the eyes develops crow's-feet. That's why even at an early age you should begin to use a moisturizer in the eye area or a mild lubricant eye cream to prevent or to slow down the appearance of lines there.

Q. How can I keep my lipstick from running into little vertical lines around my lips?

A. Apply your foundation with a sponge, covering the lips. Before putting on lipstick, blot the lips with a tissue, powder lightly, then use a lip pencil along the natural contours of your lips. Then with lipstick of a similar color fill in the lip area within the pencil contours.

Q. Why does my lipstick color always change on me, getting darker or bluer?
A. Because of the acidity of your skin you may have naturally deep-colored lips. Lips that are naturally dark or brownish need a *brown-tone lipstick*. Browns, beiges, corals, apricots, peaches—colors that have no blue in them will turn less.

Q. How can I cover my freckles?
A. I don't mind freckles!! I once drew fake freckles on a *Vogue* cover because I like them. I feel that if you cover freckles with a thick foundation, or more than one coat of foundation, your whole face looks fake, chalky, coated. I don't think it's worth it, since the freckles never get completely covered anyway. They are not at all unsightly, so don't try to hide them.

Q. How should I tweeze my brows?
A. Always from the bottom. Never tweeze brows on the top unless there are some straggly hairs above. The idea is to *raise* the brows, not to lower them. Tweeze a little bit from each brow in turn so that you don't overtweeze either. And always use a good pair of tweezers that will insure a proper grasp of the hair. You don't want the hair to slip out of your tweezers and break off. Your eyebrows should be *powdered* before you tweeze them to ensure a better grasp.

Always tweeze in the *direction* that the hair grows: the left brow should be tweezed toward the left of the face and vice versa. Using a brow brush brush the brows up and down and sideways as you go along, just as a hairdresser always brushes and combs your hair in many directions when he's cutting; you want to make sure that the brows are properly brushed so that you can better see what has to be tweezed.

If you plan extensive tweezing because you haven't done it in a while, you should tweeze in the evening so that during the night the redness can disappear.

Make sure that you disinfect the area with *alcohol* or *astringent* right away. Then immediately afterward apply some lubricant.

Frequent tweezing is better than tweezing once in a while; you will have less to do all at once and are less likely to do too much. Make sure that you don't overtweeze by separating the brows too much from each other. The ideal brow is one that starts right above the inner corner of the eye.

Q. When is a beauty mask needed?

A. Whenever you want to smooth your face, relax your face or give your face a rest before a party. It is ideal in the evening before going out if you are giving yourself a facial at home and if you want to finish with the complete luxury of a mask before an evening makeup. It should be used twice a week or every other day if you wish, but certainly at least once a week.

Q. How can I avoid color buildup due to frequently repowdering my face?

A. By selecting a colorless, translucent or transparent powder. This kind of powder gives you a matte finish without color so that you can frequently powder without having a color buildup. Also, applying powder with a *brush* helps, because you *deliver* less powder to your face than with a powder puff or a cotton ball.

Q. My eyes are often bloodshot—what can I do about that?

A. Making cups with your hands, you can splash cold water on your closed eyes ten or fifteen or twenty times. Lean over the sink and do that before applying makeup. You will see that the cold water will act as a blood-vessel constrictor, shrinking the capillaries. If that is not sufficient you might want to ask your druggist to give you mild eye drops to refresh your eyes. Make sure that makeup doesn't get into your eyes, because you might develop an irritation from mascara or an eye shadow.

Q. Should I really use night cream at night?

A. Night creams don't necessarily have to be used at night. They can very well be used during the day while you do chores or take a bath before retiring, while you're at home watching television or doing your homework—*wonderful* times when you *don't* have to look your prettiest and can afford to have a greasier face and have on a good coat of night cream. Just as long as you have a couple of hours of lubrication, I don't care if you use it in the morning or afternoon. In fact, at night you may not want to go to bed with so much on your face and a light moisturizer might be more in order then.

Q. At what age should a girl start wearing makeup?

A. Whenever she doesn't look like a baby any longer. I hate to see a very young baby face smothered in makeup. Whenever a girl looks like a young adolescent, a *light* makeup will be in order, beginning with some mascara and eye shadow. Of course the precise time should vary with the individual. You can have a very immature thirteen-year-old girl who looks sixteen, and it's quite in order for her to use makeup if she needs it.

Q. How can I protect my skin against the sun?

A. By applying a sun filter before you expose your bare skin directly to the sun. Even more than one application of a sun filter would be in order, particularly on those areas that burn the fastest, such as the décolletage, the nose, the lids, the top of the cheek-bones, under the eyes, on the very delicate eye area, the shoulders or the backs of the arms. But the face is what concerns me the most because sunburn is very painful and it's aging.

So lots of protection should be put on even *before* you go into the sun. Repeat the lotion in half an hour, when you're in the sun; then frequently reapply protective creams. After the second application you no longer have to use a sun-filter lotion; you can apply a *cream*, and *heavy lubricants* are very much recommended. The times of exposure must be watched; you have to use common sense. I'm all for the sun—as long as you take it intelligently.

As soon as you go indoors remove the cream or lotion with a *hot* towel. The hot towel over hot skin may burn at first, but it helps to take the sting away. Then follow with an immediate application of an eight-hour cream lubricant, which will relieve a mild burn if you have been unlucky enough to get one.

Q. I have blue eyes. Why don't I like the look of blue eye shadow on me?

A. Because it is wrong, and you are right! In fact, very often women try to match eye shadow to the color of their eyes, but unless you have gray hair, a *contrasting* shade would be better. If you have a bit of gray in your hair it's quite all right to use some blue eye shadow. But usually blue eye shadow looks too obvious with blue eyes. It would be better to use gray shadow or plum. These colors are much more subtle and are less obvious shades for blue eyes.

Q. Why is my nose always shiny although the rest of my face is dry?

A. Because you have more oil glands on your nose than you may have elsewhere on your face. Scrub an oily nose with astringent applications. Avoid creams on your nose. The skin on your nose never ages, so it doesn't have to be lubricated. Limit the amount of moisturizer before makeup, and when you choose makeup, be sure that the foundation you apply on the center of your face is water-based if possible, or has only a limited amount of oil in it. Frequent blotting with rice paper tissue or a light powder will remove the greasy look from the nose without upsetting the makeup on the rest of the face.

Q. Can I increase the length of my lashes?

A. You can help the growth of the lashes by using some special lubricant such as an 8-hour cream or a European cream. (French and Italian women say such a cream helps the growth of their lashes.) Try a touch of *castor oil*. Shake the open bottle onto a fingertip, catch the drop that falls and spread it between two fingers, then touch the fingers to the tips of your lashes. The castor oil will reach the roots of the lashes and encourage the growth. The castor oil application should be used in the evening before bedtime.

Q. I use moisturizer, antiwrinkle lotion and all-day cream under my foundation and my face is always very oily-looking.

A. You use too many things. After you have used cleansing cream and skin lotion it should be enough to use *either* a moisturizer *or* a daytime cream, because one has the same effect as the other. Use the wrinkle lotion *only* on those lined areas, such as at the sides of your lips, the contour of the jawline, around the eyes, perhaps around the forehead, but don't use it all over.

Q. How many different lipsticks do I *really* have to have?

A. You can get along very well with just three colors: one for the day, a light shade, with a touch of brown, perhaps, or rose—not too loud; a more intense one for the evening, which should be darker or brighter, and either redder or pinker, depending on your coloring; and if you tan, a more coral or an orangey shade.

You can then elaborate on the basic three by having a light pink for the morning, a bright red for night and a peach for the summer. You can go slowly from three to five to six, according to the extent of your wardrobe.

Q. I like to use soap and water on my face—is it bad?

A. It used to be terrible when soaps were of poor quality. Many of today's soaps are superfatted, not as drying as they were formerly, and do therapeutic things to your skin as you wash. So it isn't *as* bad providing you use a nondrying, neutral soap and *only* if you don't have dry skin. Dry skin should not know soap. It's recommended only for an oily skin.

Q. What should I do if my face perspires a lot?

A. It does? A face never perspires, a face glows. I would say that a horse sweats, a truckman perspires—but a woman glows! In any case, if you *think* you perspire, it's because you have used too much moisturizer *or* you have oily skin with oily pores *or* you drink too much water and you retain too much fluid *or* you forget to use a *mild astringent before* your makeup. In fact, there are some remarkable lotions that guarantee a smooth skin if you use them before makeup because they act on the oil glands of the face and limit the facial perspiration.

Q. Why does my foundation change its color on me?

A. Because of the acidity of your skin. It probably gets more orangey—the most common problem. Make sure that there isn't an orange base to your foundation; peach shades, for instance, are to be avoided. It's better to use *beiges*: you never go wrong with a beige or a light tan. Again, use a mild astringent, which will neutralize the acid effect of the skin and make it possible for the foundation to stay fresh.

Q. How can I correct my round face?

A. Not with makeup. At least not in my opinion. I don't approve of cheek-shading, because if you have a round face with brown shading on it, it will always remain a round face with brown on it but not a thinner-looking face.

I suggest you reconsider the shape of your *hairdo*, because the hair, having volume, will help minimize the size of the face or give the illusion of correcting its shape.

Q. What can I do to de-emphasize the length of my face?

A. By the application of rouge in the *middle* of the cheeks and perhaps by wearing bangs. Bangs, going straight down or to the side, will cut the length of a face. Three areas make up the proportions of a face: from the hairline to the brows; from the eyebrows to the upper lip; and from the upper lip to the chin. If we eliminate one of these areas by some sort of covering, the remaining two-thirds make a less long face.

Q. How can I minimize a large nose?

A. You could consider applying corrective makeup to the nose, as is often suggested in makeup pages in beauty magazines, but this involves dreadful complications that I don't believe in. I feel that if you shade your nose you achieve very little other than a peculiar-looking nose that you can't even touch or blow. I really don't believe in correcting a nose. If it is quite an impossible nose, you can consider surgery, but before you do that you should try to emphasize your *cheekbones* with rouge, emphasize your *eyes* and get the most out of them, and maybe try having a hairdo that may be just a bit higher. *Balance* is more in order than corrective makeup.

Q. Can I do anything to de-emphasize my square jaw?

A. You can have a great haircut, a wonderful pageboy with two *guiches* coming forward on your cheeks, which will be thus covered; your ears will be covered, and your hair will swing and hit right at the jawline, minimizing it.

Q. What about my very high forehead?

A. I don't mind it, because in Italy a high forehead has always been considered a sign of intelligence. In every Renaissance painting the women were portrayed with very high foreheads, perhaps framed with braids and strings of jewels. You don't want to do that of course, but please don't feel that a high forehead should be such a problem. Again, bangs will help, or having a side part or parting your hair in the middle and keeping it in place with two barrettes.

Q. What can I do for protruding eyes?

A. Avoid light eye-shadow colors. They are really the worst things you can wear. Always use dark colors: plums, browns, grays—the murky shades. A brown or any dark color de-emphasizes and minimizes; a light one will bring the eyes out even farther.

Q. What can I do about eyes that are set too close together?

A. Try to widen your eyebrows a little. If it looks right, try tweezing between them to give an illusion of a more severe, broader forehead. Then use light eye shadow in the inner corner of the eye and darker eye shadow on the outer half of the lid. This gives an illusion of eyes that are more apart. Of course you don't want to have a demarcation line in the middle of your lid, so blend one color into another as carefully as you can; the colors should go from beige to brown, for instance, or from paler green to darker green. Then make sure that the color of the outer corner also goes under the outer corner lashes of the bottom lid, as that too helps to bring the eyes farther apart. By the same token, when you are applying mascara, apply more of it on the outer lashes, and never in the inner corner. Very often applying a few false individual lashes at the outer corner helps too.

Q. How can I hide age spots?

A. With a very light foundation and a concealing cream.

First I apply the foundation all over with a sponge, then I brush the concealing cream on the spots directly; with the sponge I pat very lightly to even out the cream so that you don't have a spot showing. Cover with another dot of concealer and then a very light powder application. Of course never try to use a lighter covering; spots, like discolorations and circles, are best covered by using something that is just a shade *darker*.

Q. Does face powder help foundation last?

A. Yes. Face powder, by setting the foundation, encourages it not to melt and crease into lines as readily as it would without powder.

Q. Where exactly should rouge be applied?

A. As high as possible on the cheekbones. *Pretend* that you are drawing a line down the cheeks from the outer corner of the eye and another line that runs across from the nostrils. Wherever those two lines meet is usually your cheekbone. You can see the cheekbone when you smile; you can feel it with your fingers. Go right under the cheekbone, and blend up diagonally toward the temple; that's the best way to apply rouge.

Q. Why does my makeup fade so quickly? In a few hours I look as though I have nothing on.

A. Because you have oily skin, which absorbs makeup faster than dry skin. Always carry a sponge and your foundation in your purse, and as often as you have to, refresh the foundation with a sponge application. Reapply some rouge, just powder your nose, and you have freshened up your face.

Q. Should I use foundation when I'm tan?

A. In most cases it's not necessary. The tan makes you look so much healthier and prettier and glowing that you really don't need very much foundation. But if you are a foundation user, or if you have to use it because of discolorations that show even when you're tan, you must use a *dark* foundation over your dark tan. Always use one shade darker than your usual foundation. There is nothing worse than seeing a tanned face trying to look a shade lighter—it looks chalky.

Q. What makeup do you recommend for blond eyebrows and lashes?

A. I don't mind blond eyebrows. I often bleach eyebrows, as I believe light brows are always more flattering. They leave more of the eyes to be seen. Of course if light brows upset you, there are two things that you can do. Choose a pencil, a soft crayon in a blond or brown shade. With a little eyebrow brush, work over the lead of the pencil and then simply brush it onto your brows for a hint of color.

Or else you can apply some pencil to your brows directly, but not too heavily, then touch them with your fingers to make sure that it's not too much. As an extreme last resort you can consider dyeing your eyebrows—but please, never dark brown or black, always a *soft dark blond* or *light brown*.

For your lashes mascara is the answer. You can mascara your lashes, first on the top, and then from underneath, so that you completely coat the lashes. When you look down, the roots of your lashes won't show blond. And you can always consider dyeing your lashes, which is easily done in many beauty shops. Even if you are a platinum blonde, I don't mind if your lashes are dyed black or dark brown—and that will help you avoid using mascara so often. It's a great thing for the beach, for the summer, when you can swim without mascara on and still have dark lashes.

Q. What's the best way to remove mascara?

A. With an eye makeup pad or eye makeup removing lotion. With the eyes closed, apply a saturated pad or cotton ball and, keeping the eyes closed, loosen the mascara with little shaking motions of the pad, and then open the eyes. Remove the mascara from underneath the eyes by looking down and brushing the lashes away from the skin with the same pad or lotion. You may want to repeat the application twice. Always rinse your eyes with cold water when you have finished.

Q. How can I improve the shape of my lips?

A. By using a light-brown or brick- or sepia-colored pencil to outline the lips before the lipstick is applied. If you want to improve your lips because they are thin, you can do this to give the impression of a better body or contour to the lips. I really discourage going out of your contour with pencil because it always shows what one is trying to do and the result isn't too appealing. Improve the look of the mouth by being very careful about the lipstick application and making sure that you always have impeccable, well groomed lips.

Q. What kind of makeup do you recommend for someone wearing glasses?

A. Lenses, whether clear or slightly tinted, will hide your eyes. (I do prefer the lightly tinted ones.) Therefore your eyes must make an effect from behind the lenses, and in order to do that they must be *completely contoured with color.* Not only should much *eye shadow* be used on the top lid but a similar shade of *pencil* should be used underneath the bottom lashes so that the eyes are totally surrounded with color and floating in it. Mascara should be used abundantly on both upper and lower lashes. Eye liner can be considered for the top lid and then pencil used inside the lower lid. Always use a medium-dark eye shadow, particularly when the lens is a little tinted. (You can afford to have more going on behind your lenses than you would if the lens were a light or a clear one.) Remember total contouring, so that the eyes project through the lenses.

Q. How can I keep foundation from getting on my collars and necklines?

A. By stopping at the jawline. It's the only intelligent way to use foundation. Make sure you use a foundation that more or less matches your neck. Even if your neck is sallow, use a beige foundation, so that you don't see the demarcation line. Of course, using a sponge is the secret, so that you can blend the foundation into nothingness and you will not have foundation on your neck, which should not be made up (unless it's for a total décolleté for evening). For the day it's not necessary.

Q. Is it okay to keep on using my old sponges after they've been stained with the foundation?

A. Yes, because when they're a little older they become softer and more pliable. Actually, they're good to use until the day they just disintegrate and you have to throw them away! All you have to do after you use the sponge is wash it with soap and water and let it dry in the air, maybe just setting it on a tissue. Color stains are quite all right if the sponge has been thoroughly washed.

Q. I have very straight lashes. Will I damage them by using an eyelash curler?

A. If you use it intelligently, probably not. I don't mind straight lashes because I've seen many bad results from using the eyelash curler indiscriminately. I feel that if you are very careful you can use it; otherwise, why don't you just consider using two coats of mascara? Bend the lashes back for a few seconds with the wand or brush while the mascara dries, and that will probably make your lashes somewhat less straight.

Q. What can I do to hide a blemish or pimple or skin discoloration such as brown spots due to using the pill or circles under the eyes?

A. The answer to all of these problems is a clever, careful use of a concealing cream. You can apply it with your little finger around the eyes so that you hide your circles; you can pat it onto a brown spot with a finger, then blend with the sponge if you have to: Or you can use a concealing cream with the help of a brush and simply paint your pimple with it and then make sure that there is no contour showing, always by patting with the finger or sponge. In fact, you should reapply the concealing cream where there is a pimple or a discoloration. One application won't do because the first one only begins to hide the blemish; reapply the cream for the best cover.

Q. Why are my eyes always puffy in the morning?

A. Probably you are retaining fluid. It might be a good idea to check with your doctor to see if there is anything that he can do for you. But from a makeup point of view, just splash your eyes with cold water, and don't apply your makeup right away. When we wake up, the face is apt to be puffy, like the body, and groggy. So you have to wait until the body and the face both wake up. Eyes are never puffy at night because we *live* through the day.

Q. What is the safest way to remove hair from the upper lip?

A. My suggestion is lip wax, but I disapprove of waxing on the face other than on the upper lip. I think one should wax the legs, the underarms, arms, but not the face. Nor do I like to use facial depilatories, because although they are a fast and safe way, they are not an intelligent way, since you get rid of hair only on the surface. You leave the follicles untouched, so the hair grows right back. The treatment doesn't at all discourage the growth. I think that the wax is the most logical way to get rid of unwanted hair in this spot. If it is a really serious problem for you, consult a professional about electrolysis.

Q. Can I quickly reduce the size of my pores?

A. Large pores take a very long time to minimize. To correct this condition, you have to use a very light, nongreasy foundation, very light, effective penetrating moisturizer (not thick lubricants, which would cause further opening of the pores) and frequent astringent applications and astringent refreshing masks. But please do not expect immediate and miraculous results—the process is a long one.

Q. Do you approve of false eyelashes for daytime?

A. Not particularly. I think that false eyelashes are all right at night, if perfectly applied. During the day you wear a skirt and a shirt or a sweater for a casual look. The evening hours are the time when makeup should be more exciting, and lashes are one of those evening additions that make all the difference. But I don't think that one should ever allow fake lashes to look fake. They should simply add to the thickness of your own lashes rather than to the length. In other words, use lashes for fullness. To give a further illusion of thickness, you may want to apply eyeliner to your eyes as I have discussed in "A Look at the Eyes." Use the eyeliner at the root of your lashes to emphasize the thickness, making sure that there is a bit of liner at the beginning and at the end of the lid, so that the strip does not sit on a bare lid.

Q. How can I correct my ruddy complexion?

A. By toning it down with a beige foundation.

Q. My complexion is too sallow and I don't look right with a rosy foundation color.

A. The reason a rosy foundation looks wrong is that a sallow complexion with a rose or pink or peach foundation becomes a rosy face over a yellow neck. Choose a beige foundation; with beige you cannot go wrong. Don't ask your foundation to correct the sallowness of your face—ask your *blusher* to do this. Blusher or cream rouge or dry rouge will help a great deal to correct sallowness by adding healthy highlights.

Q. Should the foundation for night be lighter or darker than what I generally use during the day?

A. I prefer to think that a woman looks a little more fragile, a little more romantic, a little more refined at night, so I suggest in most cases that she use a lighter foundation at night. During the day you can use a shade darker to emphasize a fading tan or look outdoorsy. But if you are quite dressed up, use a shade lighter and wear a bright cheek rouge.

Q. In what order should makeup be applied?

A. The foundation first, then the cheek color, next the eyes, and last the lips—the order we have followed throughout the book. (Remember: after lipstick is put on, recheck your rouge to see if you want to apply some more.)

Q. What is the right makeup for my wedding day?

A. Every woman is ready to take all the time she needs to look her best on this most important day. But often a woman makes the mistake of overusing makeup, finishing with an unnatural look that is not right for her on this occasion.

I think that the groom is often lost sight of. He wants to see the girl he chose to marry, not someone who, because of makeup, looks strange to him.

My approach to makeup for your wedding day is the believable approach you take every other day of your life. Perhaps you will want to use a lighter foundation and less rouge to give the impression of utter serenity. The look you want is a clear one. I love to see a translucent quality on a bride's face, with no noticeable makeup to come between her and the meaning of her day.

I see a light makeup, with just a hint of a blush. You want to look pretty; today is not the day to strive for glamor or an exotic look. Rather, you want to look like a fine porcelain princess. A man is always shy about makeup, particularly when it's on the woman he loves. Confronting him with a made-up look is the wrong way to start your marriage. (There will be plenty of time for surprises later!)

This day calls for a dewy freshness, for a blush of innocence, and above all, for the appearance of the same girl he courted—a girl, I hope, who became an expert at the ten-minute makeup miracle. That's the image you want to project on this day and on every other day of your life!

CHAPTER FIFTEEN

Famous Faces

There will always be disagreements as to which woman's face is most famous, but as to where to find famous faces, the answer is indisputable. Famous faces are in the news. The images of these women fill the gossip columns and the society columns. They are well known because of their family names or their wealth, because they are fashion-setters or international jet-setters, because they have great talent or just because they are terrific hostesses.

They have realized the dream of ordinary people: to be instantly recognizable and to be sought after and photographed—which spells success. These celebrated women all have in common a quality that sets them apart: individualism. They are each remarkable, different from all other women. They each have a look and a personality which create an unforgettable face. Rather than try to change their features, these women have capitalized on their natural endowments. They are considered extraordinary beauties, though less than one percent of the faces I will discuss could really be described as "perfect." This is why I don't try to correct flaws. I believe that flaws can be turned into assets if you know how to work around them. The following women prove my point.

Jacqueline Kennedy Onassis is a woman who possesses a very special bone structure. Her face—rounder when she was younger—has become thinner, emphasizing her high, wide-set cheekbones. With such an asset one already is outstanding. It's great to have that kind of bone structure along with a terrific complexion and very good, dark hair.

Her eyes are very far apart and tend to look small. She wears very little eye makeup, preferring to accent the eyes with sunglasses. Wearing brown shadow to the bone below the brows would be a definite plus, as well as using a brown pencil underneath the bottom lashes.

Jackie, with her bright, open smile and her huge sunglasses, has accepted her looks and has made the most of a face that isn't perfectly beautiful. Her smile and sunglasses have become her trademark, proving that you can be smashing without being a great beauty. She is the perfect example of self-acceptance.

Self-acceptance is just what the word implies—accepting the way you look and making the most of it without trying to alter your features in any way. For Jacqueline Onassis that means ruling out plastic surgery as well as the less drastic measures such as shading and contouring. She has defied the norm, telling the world that it had better love her as she is, and the world has listened to her! This is a lesson everyone can learn.

Diahann Carroll has one of the most beautiful faces I've ever seen. I often work with her and have always admired her great professionalism. She radiates grace, in her sweet voice, her hands and her entire body. She's an absolutely lovely woman and has great talent.

She always knows what is going to look right or wrong and she instinctively chooses what's right for her. Her makeup is always correct because she understands that a woman should never overdo.

Diahann takes extra-special care of her complexion. Hers is a combination skin type, with dry areas around the eyes and rather oily, open pores on her nose and chin. She uses astringent on her nose and chin and often relaxes for a few minutes with a thin pad of saturated cotton wool over these areas to minimize the pores. A large amount of lubricant is slathered on her eye area at the same time, counteracting the tendency to develop lines.

Diahann is always perfectly made up. She knows that an almost black eye shadow is the best way to make her very dark eyes come alive—it's a wonderful way to make the eyes look smoky and sensuous. She wears false lashes, but they are of the correct length and texture. Her lips are of a perfect design and she loves bright-red lipsticks, a glorious contrast to her brown complexion.

She used to be a strong believer in shading her cheekbones to make her face look less round. Though she always looked just as

beautiful without any shading, it was a security blanket that many actresses have, left over from her earlier days. She, like many others, was probably told that it was necessary in order to photograph better. It's a hard habit to break. But with today's concept that less is more, shading can be forgotten unless it's used to correct very definite flaws, which Diahann Carroll doesn't have. She now uses shading only for extreme harsh camera lighting.

Arlene Dahl is really one of the most beautiful, serene women in the world. Her tremendous honesty and *joie de vivre* has given her the strength to get through many worries in her private and professional lives. Her small forehead is without a line, as though no worry ever crossed her mind. When she talks to you her voice is like a sweet mountain stream, filled with musical notes.

Her professional training has carried over into her private life. What she learned as an actress she practices as a businesswoman. And what a beautiful one! Her hair is the fabulous color of cognac, so very flattering to her. Her Scandinavian background gave her a

lovely peaches-and-cream complexion, which is so pale that spending even a day in the sun would be disastrous. She nurtures that skin with a thorough maintenance program. She'll never go to sleep with as much as a speck of makeup still on her face. Her pores are very refined and she is never without a moisturizer on her face. She believes in a great deal of beauty rest and gives her face constant attention.

When it comes to makeup, Arlene knows where to stop. Her sensuous mouth, accented by that famous birthmark, gets a bright, shiny lipstick, a terrific contrast to her fair skin and her pale brows. She prefers to concentrate on her unbelievable eyes. She realizes that though her eyes are a beautiful blend of gray and blue, they still need contouring, as they are pale. Her upper lashes are heavily mascara'ed. She also applies a set of very, very fine and well cut false lashes to the bottom ones, giving her that starry, open-eyed quality I love. Her eyes become two jewels, exquisitely centered and mounted.

Sophia Loren has one of the great faces of the century. Her face will go down in history as being remarkable and unforgettable, although she started as a rather common-looking girl. She had, nevertheless, very good bone structure, long legs, a curvaceous body and a very fine complexion, a generous smile, and thick, dark hair—on the whole, a look that was very much appreciated in those postwar films she made in Italy. But her looks were slightly plebeian. The women she usually portrayed were not greatly sophisticated. In fact, in one movie she played the part of a grande dame with a Rolls Royce and just didn't look right; she wasn't believable. But when, in the same film, she played a woman of the ghetto, with seven children, she was truly superb. This hadn't really to do with her face, but rather with her background.

There is a reason for every wrinkle we have, a reason that we mature into someone different and distinct from all others, a reason for what we become and how we look. And Sophia had a very difficult life. When she married well she took on a whole new dimension and began working on her looks. I remember how the change came about from a pretty peasant girl to a stunning, gracious woman.

She concentrated on her eyes, making them doelike and elongated by adopting that famous "brown eye," making the most of her upper lids. She bleached her eyebrows and tweezed them. She abandoned lipstick in favor of a brown contouring pencil and lots of gloss to enhance her full lips. All of this created an unforgettable face.

Now Sophia Loren has that wonderful self-assurance in regard to her nose. Although she won't be photographed in profile, she refuses to change it. Though she keeps the less-than-perfect nose from the camera as much as possible, you can still see that glorious face and remember how much of a part her vibrant personality plays.

Gloria Vanderbilt Cooper is a very strong individual, a woman determined to succeed in everything she undertakes, from her fashion-designing to her art work. What I like about her face is its one-of-a-kind quality. She's very pale, yet it works for her. Though I usually go for a tanned look, I love seeing her skin so pearly white. She's unique and sensational. That creamy complexion is enhanced by her black hair and her dark brows. Her small eyes are dark, with a strong, piercing quality. She has full lips and uses bright lipstick which brightens her entire face. A room fills with light when she switches on her incredible smile.

Gloria's grooming is impeccable. She takes terrific care of herself and is a living proof that you can work and have children and still maintain a young, healthy figure—as long as you have sufficient help at home. Her secret is walking, and she does it beautifully and proudly, throwing one leg in front of the other in a stunning stride, tall and erect. Her beauty regime reflects that kind of simplicity. She wears little makeup and shuns frivolous hair styles, preferring to pull her hair back or wear it short and parted in the center. Skin care is also very important to her.

Gloria Vanderbilt Cooper has a famous name, a famous face and lots of money, and yet she's a working woman and a stylish woman—a total success.

Maria Callas. One of the most noted women of our time. The older she got the more attractive she became. An incredible performer who used every part of her body onstage, like perhaps no other soprano, and whose voice was one of the most celebrated in the world. A voice has to be trained, she said, or else it will leave you. The same goes for good looks. You have to train yourself to keep your looks if you want to be good-looking longer. You must work at your skin constantly and be meticulous about your makeup as Maria was.

She was one of the first prima donnas to lose weight, and with the weight loss her face became more striking and more beautiful than ever. Although she looked wonderful with a tan, she seldom went into the sun, preferring a very pale, quiet beige foundation to play down her strong, dark looks. Rouge on her cheeks gave her a glow without overemphasizing her naturally good cheekbones. She toned down her full lips, selecting the palest pinks and peaches, the lightest, most neutral lipstick colors of the palette.

Maria had masses and masses of dark-auburn hair, most often pulled back or twisted into a simple chignon at the nape of her neck to emphasize her small ears.

It would have been easy for Maria to look like a lion, particularly onstage, but she shunned such an obvious look. Instead her eye

makeup was understated. She used only the smallest amount of turquoise eye shadow, a color that worked surprisingly well for her. She applied just enough to lighten her dark eyes. Onstage she used eyeliner dramatically, but in private life she applied a thin line of dark brown, stopping at the outer corners, just enough to emphasize the almond shape of her eyes. She used plenty of mascara, and she loved to use the pencil inside and under the bottom lid, totally encircling her eyes.

Maria was a great loss to those of us who knew and loved her, and to millions more who knew only her talent.

Barbara Walters is a woman of many accomplishments, most notably a successful career, an exciting life style and a look that's all her own. She's one of the most highly paid TV personalities in the world, and although she's not a great beauty, she's much more than an average brunette. She has put together a look of her own—one that balances her strong eyes and her bright, full mouth—and she's determined to make it stick. Barbara is very conservative and reluc-

tant to change her looks if she feels she'll become too flamboyant. This conservatism stems from the fact that she's on television daily and is leery of viewer response. If she trimmed her brows she would call more attention to her eyes. More eye makeup would take emphasis away from her full mouth, but then she would run into the problem of looking too made up. After all, she is a reporter, not an actress. Her makeup must reflect that life style.

Barbara does take excellent care of her skin, rotating night creams and lubricants—as I often suggest—to keep the skin more responsive, so it won't become immune to the same kind of cream day in and day out.

I most admire what Barbara has done for eyeglass wearers. Hers always look charming and fashionable. Her frames are large and the lenses are tinted, making Barbara look beautifully accessorized. This is just one facet of this thoroughly together woman.

Faye Dunaway. The first thing that comes to mind is just how good-looking she is. Hers is the most symmetrically perfect face to come into the limelight of late. Her cheekbones are very, very high, and the planes of her face are very interesting. I am talking about a woman who is certainly petite, yet so perfectly proportioned that her small stature goes unnoticed. Her looks are impressive because of their versatility. According to the makeup she uses or the part she is playing, she can be a glamorous, innocent or exotic beauty.

When I saw her recently I realized that her makeup needs were a little more complex than the public may have imagined. She needs little makeup, but it must be perfectly applied, otherwise it looks like overkill. Mistakes would be sorely obvious on her strong face.

Her skin is kept flawless by a very thin moisturizing foundation. She wears makeup only at night and when she is working; during the day, she wears no makeup at all.

She has marvelous teeth and looks young and innocent when she goes without lipstick. When she colors her mouth with a bright or a dark shade she immediately becomes sophisticated; her mouth becomes more important and her teeth look like wonderful pearls. I like what she does with her rather pointed upper lip which is shaped like an M. She emphasizes those two points with a pencil, a brick-

or brown- or scarlet-colored one, depending on the shade of lipstick she'll follow with. The lip is better defined, and the lipstick is better defined and less likely to run, particularly with the great amount of gloss she uses on top.

She has a natural hollow under those terrific cheekbones and doesn't need any shading or contouring. Faye uses a lot of rouge, in cream form, and then a blusher. This healthy color lights up her face. There is almost no powder in her regime, aside from the toning down of her forehead sheen, next to the hairline and around her perfectly proportioned nose.

The space between the lashes and the eyebrows is very exciting

on Faye's face. She uses a great deal of brown eye shadow on the lid and a lighter shade in the inner corner of her eyes to make them look farther apart. Her eyes are brown, and she favors the subtle tones of brown shadows rather than a stronger, overpowering color. Because of a protruding eyebrow bone she fully recognizes the need of shading with brown shadow, blended all the way to the brows. Her eyebrows are very thin; she has learned to keep them trimmed to a minimum. To enhance the arch she uses a very light amount of blond pencil—the minimum in brow makeup.

Faye happens to have very good lashes, which she curls and loads with mascara. (She never wears false lashes.) She uses a brown pencil to give the illusion of fuller bottom lashes and also to help open the eyes vertically.

She has a marvelous face that one can learn a lot from.

*F*arrah *Fawcett-Majors.* Ever since the time of Jean Harlow, the Platinum Blonde of the Thirties, there has almost always been a reigning golden girl in American popular culture. Without a Harlow or a Lana Turner or a Marilyn Monroe, our landscape has always seemed a little bleak. No one filled the space left by Marilyn's untimely death until Farrah Fawcett-Majors. In the past year she has captured our imagination and thus occupied the throne reserved for America's blonde goddess, the number one glamor girl.

Like her predecessors, Farrah has truly remarkable hair, an asset carefully exploited. Her fabulous mane, which has been meticulously streaked and cut, is the immediate attraction. It frames and counterpoints a flashing smile. This combination is irresistible, defining a face that everyone wants to look at. When she looks straight at you with her sparkling eyes, she has an American look that is so appealing one never tires of it. There is a basic wholesomeness about her that fits the standard of contemporary beauty, a turning away from the artifice and exaggeration of the past yet without a resort to gimmickry.

I find her makeup flawless because she has studied her face and knows it very well. The look is so right for her that it is difficult to

imagine her any other way—with pulled-back hair and glasses, for example. She uses brown bronze eye shadow, which creates a wonderful contrast with her enamel-blue eyes. The exaggerated amount of mascara she wears, together with a few extra lashes added here and there, contributes to making her eyes brilliant and gemlike. She would look better, however, with less shading on her cheeks, which is probably a left-over-from-TV concept that shouldn't be continued with away from the cameras and lights.

Farrah's hairstyle has made her the most influential of all stars in getting other women to accept, and love, the natural, free-flowing, unconstructed look that I find so marvelous. This hairdo is based on superb cutting, so skillfully done that the hair falls always into natural lines, and looks good even in a windstorm! This to me is a welcome, *freeing* beauty development that is so much more elegant in the true sense than those stiff, elaborate don't-dare-touch-me coiffures that one still sees, lacquered and sprayed to a fare-thee-well.

Farrah is today's version of sexiness, a departure from the voluptuous curves and tape-breaking measurements of the glamor girls of the recent past. This too I find refreshing. She radiates a natural sensuality that is contemporary and completely captivating.

Raquel Welch definitely has one of the greatest figures in Hollywood. She's a very beautiful woman, with remarkable legs, lovely shoulders—a perfect body. Her face is a work of art because she takes a great deal of time to apply her makeup. She's a perfectionist and has a beauty kit that's as nearly complete as it could be.

Her eyes are cleverly made up with all-brown shadowing, brown from the crease all the way up to the eyebrows to give that beautiful depth to the eye. She loves to play down the bone over her eyebrow, so she carefully powders that area with invisible powder so that there won't be any shine. She brushes up her brows and fills them in with light strokes.

I was pleased to have been able to bleach her brows lightly. I believe that the less you notice the brow, the more you notice the eye. Her brows were made one shade lighter than the hair, and the look was wonderful.

Raquel applies a dot of eyeliner in the inner and outer corners of her eyes. She applies bottom lashes one by one, which opens her eyes tremendously. On the upper lid she should use a thinner, more believable false lash than she does on the screen. She knows what she's doing, which is why her makeup is perfect.

She is careful in the shading of her cheeks, so that her glorious

face is always open and natural-looking. Although there is a great deal going on in terms of makeup, it is all done in small, invisible touches. She is just as meticulous when shading her lips to make them look fuller. Her loving care has made her terrific face such a success.

***T**he Duchess of Windsor* is a real example of painstakingly careful discipline in grooming, a woman who was never a great beauty but who has always had sublime taste. Her skin has always been pretty and her eyes very alive. She has had the great fortune to be slim enough to wear every fashion. Her famous statement "A woman can never be too thin or too rich," explains her maintaining a very firm diet and a severe beauty routine. No matter how tired she would be after a social function, she would still spend an hour on her special exercises, skin-care treatments and makeup-removal steps before retiring. Her skin has remained impeccable because of that care.

She developed one famous hairdo, the one with the part in the middle and the bouffant sides, which always leaves the ears uncovered, so that her thin face seems a little larger. The hair is always well trimmed and up in the back to make her neck look longer. Her makeup is kept to a minimum. She loves bright lipstick and very little eye makeup.

I think that I was the first to persuade her to apply false eyelashes in the sixties, when Miss Arden was still alive. I had been sent to her suite at the Waldorf Astoria, to give her a makeup consultation. I arrived, very excited, with one pair of false eyelashes in my makeup kit.

I finally convinced her to wear them. She was all giggles because she had never tried them before and she wondered whether or not His Highness would approve. (He was needlepointing in the next room while I was making her up.) I started clipping the two strips of lashes, and one fell to the floor. The carpeting was brown and I couldn't find it. I was getting very upset and nervous because I had only one lash strip left in my hand. The other was hopelessly lost. We rang for the chambermaid, who looked all over but couldn't find it. The Duchess volunteered to look, but we didn't want her to get down on the floor. The Duke was called. He put down the needlepoint, came in and started looking on his hands and knees with a flashlight, but he couldn't find it. I had to come up with a quick solution.

"But of course you wouldn't want to wear lashes if they looked false on. I'll tell you how we're going to cope with this," I said.

I proceeded to cut the remaining lash strip into sections, which I then applied here and there. And that was the beginning of individual lashes applied one by one! I invented the method out of sheer desperation, having to make one lash strip do for two eyes. But the end result was pleasing and is really the best way to approach false lashes, since you don't want an obvious look.

I just want you to know that later that day, when I went home and had my clothes ironed, the lash was found in a trouser cuff.

The Duchess was so pleased with the results of the consultation that she wrote a wonderful letter of praise to Miss Arden. Her makeup had to be very discreet because of her fine complexion and her delicate features. She wouldn't look right with a stronger, vampish type of makeup.

Her good cheekbones are emphasized by the slightest amount of pink blusher, a color I don't always like, but which looked right on her. I used a bright, light lipstick, though I suspect she made it darker when I left. The eye makeup I selected was very discreet and natural, a very pale blue-gray shadow on the lid and blue pencil inside and underneath the bottom lid. Her eyes are hazel, but at times they turn blue-gray. Multicolored eyes always look better with color underneath as well as above. The Duchess' makeup is always very, very light. She has a very good complexion which should never be smothered under a heavy makeup.

I think it's terrific that she has never considered her high, high forehead as a flaw and never thought of changing her hair style or adopting bangs to hide the forehead. On the contrary, she made it higher still by pushing her hair back, away from her face. She showed that the moment you decide to believe in something, you should totally support your point of view. If you hold onto your belief firmly, that aspect of your appearance will become your trademark, just like that of the Duchess of Windsor, who created an image of refinement and good grooming that will always be hers.

Diana Vreeland has one of the most interesting faces in the world. Here is a woman over seventy who for many years was the editor in chief of *Bazaar* and then *Vogue* and who is currently the head of the Costume Institute at the Metropolitan Museum of Art. A woman of great interest. A woman who has the very rare quality of making those she listens to feel alive and bright and interesting. A woman who is always curious about life and interested in what she's doing.

One second she'll be talking to a world-renowned doctor, the next minute to a hairdresser, the next hour to a modern sculptor, the next day to a rock star. And she'll always be interested and have something to say. That is the beauty of Diana Vreeland, that she is so involved, so alive.

There are many stories to tell about Mrs. Vreeland—for instance, that she would stand on one leg for hours at a time because she felt sure that in another life she had been a flamingo. Well, both of her legs are beautiful.

What is truly wonderful about Mrs. Vreeland is that she doesn't try to be pretty, but just to look striking.

Her makeup is heavily influenced by Japanese Kabuki theater. Her hair is jet black. Her skin is white to pink. Her cheeks are bright with rouge and her lips are bright red. But there's not one speck of eye makeup on her eyes, just a sheen of eight-hour cream on the lid—not a hint of color, just shine.

Now, isn't that a rare example of growing old with incredible intelligence and grace! She knows that she looks well in beige, red and black; you don't see much of any other color in her wardrobe. She knows that she doesn't look good with rings on her fingers, so she wears wonderful bracelets. She knows that she doesn't look good with curls, so her hair is pulled back on top and two *guiches* curl around her ears—one length, one style for years. That is imposing a style with fabulous assurance, and she has succeeded.

Lauren Hutton is the greatest example of the models' revolution that is sweeping the fashion world. She's the first to earn $200,000 a year by capitalizing on her flaws. I say it all the time. Turn your flaws into assets.

She has a crooked nose, so she smiles the other way to even out both cheeks. She has less than perfect lips, and she corrects that by a very clever application of brown pencil on one lip and gloss on the other. She has a gap between her teeth that she refuses to have fixed, so she uses a temporary cap when she knows she'll be smiling in a picture. She uses shadow to correct a bump on her nose and makes everything look fine. The flaws are all gone.

She has managed to say to the world, "I'm unique," and to tell it that hers is a highly individualized face with flaws that she accepts. The flaws are not ugly, they're simply hers, and she, rightly, chooses to keep them. She has imposed her attitude on everyone and has become a great success.

She is the living, walking proof that one does not have to be perfect to have a famous, smashing face. I admire very much her setting the example for those people who are less well endowed than others.

Lauren Hutton—a great contemporary face and person!

Marisa Berenson has stupendous eyes. The irises are colored in blended shades of green, blue, gray and gold; they are like precious stones with many different facets. She can take a lot of eye makeup, yet she looks good with only two coats of mascara and nothing else. There are few eyes that look better than hers with a large amount of blue pencil inside the bottom lid.

Her complexion is good, very good. She is blessed with beautiful skin, which is kept in perfect condition by steamings. She believes in deep cleansing of the pores, every other day, by applying hot towels, followed by a light creaming, a light soap-and-water wash, an application of astringent and, finally, a moisturizer—the ideal way to care for a complexion. She is also a great believer in masks. Marisa often uses one before an important makeup; it's the quickest way to smooth the skin and close the pores. Her complexion is certainly very well cared for.

She always wears lipstick; without it she looks washed out. And she doesn't try to make her lips look fuller than they are. She contours her lips well and uses a lot of shine on her lips as well as on lids.

Marisa's nose is not the most perfect, and she is seldom photographed in profile. But she is a living proof that by emphasizing the eyes you can give the impression of a perfect nose, even when it is far from perfect. And nobody would ever think that Marisa Berenson is less than perfection.

Goldie Hawn is a wonderful all-American doll. She has a healthy sandy-beach freshness, beautiful, remarkable eyes of the most startling blue and a very lovely body. To top it all off she has found makeup and hairdressing formulas that work perfectly for her.

Goldie Hawn will never be a sophisticated, femme-fatale kind of woman; she is a very attractive young and outdoorsy person, and

her makeup accentuates this quality. That windblown, blond hair, that bright, shiny mouth and those lovely eyes are pure Goldie. Those eyes get the most attention—from Goldie and everyone who sees her. She adds lots of individual lashes and uses a shadow that doesn't always work for most women—a frosted blue that complements her big blue eyes. This eye regime works for this enchanting blonde woman although it might look commonplace on faces that don't have her California ripe-peach naturalness.

I think that it's wonderful that she has never tried to contour or shade her full, round face. In her case, putting brown on round cheeks wouldn't make them look thinner; they would look like round cheeks with brown on them. Because she is so attractive naturally, a made-up look would be all wrong for her. Shading her face would be a definite mistake, and Goldie Hawn isn't making any mistakes.

If you have Goldie's coloring you could try out her look, adapting it to your own specific features rather than copying it precisely. It's always better to be an original than a carbon copy of someone else.

Greta Garbo and Marlene Dietrich

No discussion of famous faces would be complete without mention of the two great classic beauties Greta Garbo and Marlene Dietrich, each so different from the other, yet equally unforgettable.

When they looked down on me from the silver screen I realized that their faces were the most highly individualized. I was intrigued by their remarkable facial planes, shapes and proportions. If there was any one reason that I became involved in this business it would be my admiration for their fascinating features.

Whenever I'm making up eyes I'm sure to give them a little deeper appearance because of Garbo and Dietrich's great lids. They were so entrancing and sensual that I've always used them as a guide. Of course I don't try to copy their looks exactly, but I am certainly inspired by those two women. I think it's wonderful that Garbo and Dietrich lived and live on as models for all of us.

Greta Garbo. Hers is a most enchanting face, with those penetrating eyes, that perfect bone structure. Today Garbo cares more about her health and maintaining a fit body through exercises and nutrition, helped by her good friend and mine Gaylord Hauser. She's out in the sun a lot, though she hardly ever exposed herself to it in years past—that's how careful she was about her fine complexion. She cares little for makeup now, but in her day she inspired the *fatale*-esque look recognized the world over. She was such an important face in the movies that in Europe she was called *La Divina*, the divine one.

Her makeup was always so right for her. Her thin lips were darkened only for films. And with little makeup otherwise, she enhanced her dynamic eye lids. She was the first to wear a deep line in the crease of her lid to emphasize its spaciousness, making her eyes look even more heavy-lidded and oh so enigmatic. Her lashes were very thin. To thicken and lengthen them she applied a magically invisible set of her own fine, false lashes. Blusher on her cheeks to make them even higher gave her a glorious face that left a definite mark on all our spirits.

Marlene Dietrich. She will go down in history as having had the most special face of this century. Her features are unique: cold eyes, fine lips, a well proportioned head. And she was always so very slim.

It is said that she removed her back molars to achieve the sunken-cheek look she's so well known for. Whether or not that's true, her look has succeeded and has become a very famous, important look in the makeup world.

Her performances are always exciting because of the amount of study that goes into the preparation of her face, her body, her entire look. She has become a legend because of her marvelous legs and her strange, husky voice. She sings in that very special way that her public adores.

All of this tells you that it's important to develop a personality, one that is constructed around a special point of view, one that you will never digress from. Marlene will never experiment with different looks because she has found one that is absolutely sublime. She found a way to look unforgettable and she stuck to it. And, too, she has accepted her flaws and worked with them. Although she has thin lips, she doesn't attempt to make them look thicker or bigger. She built a strong melancholy look around them instead. If you never see Marlene Dietrich smiling, you know it's because of the specific image she created, one she developed and has upheld for more than forty years!

The Dressing Table Inventory

Just as a painter needs his brushes, paints and palette to create, so does the makeup artist. Children can manage very nicely with simple finger paints, but you don't want your face to be the product of such an unsubtle application. Your makeup approach to the priceless canvas that is your face should be sophisticated and artistic. And good makeup demands the right products and implements.

Don't be concerned that you will have to spend a great deal of money on a great many different things; this is generally not true. Beauty is luxury in the finest sense of the word, but it is definitely not an extravagance.

What I am calling the "dressing table" may not be exactly that. Most women use makeup in their bathrooms because so many products call for the rinsing of hands after application. The woman who does use a vanity or dressing table will need a small supply of water available, not only for the hands but for the wetting of sponges and dipping of brushes. I am less concerned about where you do your makeup than how you have the area organized. This is important, because good makeup can never be applied in a slapdash manner amid disorder.

Your drawers or shelves should be carefully arranged. I love those little plastic trays that have compartments for everything and fit into a drawer or right in your medicine cabinet. Tall cups that hold brushes and pencils and tubes are helpful too.

Remember that your attitude and approach are part of the magic of makeup, and though they're unseen, the results are always highly visible. If you are harassed and in turmoil when you put on your makeup, a smooth, polished look is just about impossible.

Once you have the approach and the organization, we can begin.

A glorious-looking makeup can be applied only on a thoroughly cleansed face, so we will start our inventory of beauty needs with products from the skin-care list.

Skin Care

Cleanser A younger or oilier skin would benefit most from the cleansing action of a milky, water-soluble lotion. Cleansing cream is a heavier formulation, excellent for dry or mature complexions.

Skin Lotion For oily skin, a clear, alcohol-based astringent or toner; for dry skin, a nonalcoholic lotion.

Exfoliating Lotion A toning product especially recommended for oily skin as an every-other-day pick-me-up. A dry skin that is dull or lax could benefit from once-a-week use of this liquid. It helps the skin slough off dead cells and unclogs pores, leaving the complexion tight, clear and glorious.

Moisturizer Depending on your skin type, choose from the light, whipped-creamlike consistencies to the heavier superconcentrated treatments that can penetrate up to twenty layers of skin. Everyday use, after cleansing and toning.

Eye Makeup Remover For the rather stubborn job of removing mascara. These removers—available lotions to use with cotton or as presaturated pads—are superperforming, with lubricants that are good for the skin eye of the area and for the lashes.

Masks   Have a wardrobe of masks for your every need. A peel-off mask: quick refreshment before going out; refreshing masks: a specially formulated treatment; moisturizing masks: for skin that tends to be dry; seaweed-based cream mask: for the complete half-hour luxury treatment.

Special Creams   Extra-duty creams that provide a better lubrication than moisturizer for dry skin of the entire face. "Night cream" that can be used at any hour of the day. You might like to have two to alternate between: a vitamin-based cream and a hormone cream are the best.

Multipurpose Cream   I highly recommend that every beauty inventory contain an "eight-hour" cream. This is a multipurpose product whose name refers not to the length of time it must remain on the skin but rather to the degree of effectiveness of the application. And for what does one use an eight-hour cream? Just about everything. If you burn yourself—in the kitchen or in the sun—the eight-hour cream is a wonderful remedy. It also works on windburn, for chapped lips. It's a fine cuticle cream and it's good for promoting long, lush lashes. Dab some on a pimple.

If your scalp is dry, rub a good amount of the cream into it the night before you shampoo. It makes your hair look dreadful while it's on, almost like a fright wig, but when you see and feel what it does for your hair overnight, you won't regret it.

The eight-hour cream is almost like a first-aid beauty kit in a single jar or tube.

Eye and Throat Creams   If you are a perfectionist about skin care you will want to include these two items on your list. The eye cream is a particularly rich formulation designed especially for the area just around the eyes, the very place where lines and aging show first. There is a reason for that bagging tendency; it is due to the fact that there are no oil glands below that skin surface.

The eye cream is so rich that you need only use the tiniest amount. Merely touching your finger to it is sufficient, you don't have to take any out of the jar. Just a dot on your finger, spread to another finger, and you can massage gently in the area of both eyes at once.

Throat cream is a very desirable thing, for the woman over forty or anyone at any age who feels her neck is not as firm as she'd like it to be. This specialized cream is designed to tighten up the skin on the throat.

Lash Cream   A lubricating cream for eyelashes. It makes them more elastic, less prone to breaking when you remove mascara—a luxurious extra.

Hand and Body Cream or *Lotion*   For pampering your hands and body after work, after a bath, after being outdoors. All-over benefits from constant, generous applications. Your hands especially need this extra attention. A large plastic bottle will go a long way.

Makeup

Concealing Cream   This is especially effective for covering a bump, a bruise, a discoloration or a blemish. Go under and over foundation for a trouble spot, blending thoroughly. Available in three shades, depending on your complexion: light, medium, dark.

Foundation   This is the all-important makeup, a complexion enhancer that becomes part of the complexion itself. It is available in many different formulations and shades—two are enough: a light for the evening, a shade closest to your skin tone for daytime.

Rouge   Cream rouge is the most effective and gives the most natural effect. It can be accentuated with dry brush-on blusher. For oily skin try using the blusher alone. Gels are recommended for a casual, light look in makeup. Again, only two shades are needed and should be coordinated with your foundation.

Powder   To be used sparingly and only on areas where you don't want shine—nose, forehead, chin. I recommend translucent powder for no color buildup. Available, like concealing cream, in light, medium and dark. Never use over cream rouge, but under blusher, when using that alone.

Eye Shadow Pressed powder in a compact is best for over-all color. All you need are two shades, perhaps a light and a dark variation of a color, such as a doeskin and a dark tobacco brown.

Eye Color Pencils These are great for color under the bottom lashes in places where powders can't easily reach. Match pencils to your eye-shadow shades. Have a pencil for touching up brows and lining the eyes. They're fun and versatile.

Mascara The world can't live without mascara. Nothing else does so much to dramatize the eyes. Black always, and lots of it.

Eyeliner Available as automatic liner or cake liner in a compact with brush. Use it and my smudging technique for great results. Black color here too.

False Eyelashes Use to add fullness rather than length. Have plenty of glue available when practicing—this isn't an easy job. Brown lashes only; never buy black ones.

Lip Color A basic wardrobe begins with a red, a pink and a coral. Build as you go. Brighter colors for evening, deeper colors during the day. Lipsticks are wonderful!

Lip Color Pencils These are terrific lip liners. Coordinate with your lipsticks. Remember: you can use these for cheek color too.

Lip Gloss Available in tubes, jars, pots. Have a colorless one for wearing over lipstick and a few tinted shades when going it alone. Great moisturizing effect too. Just slip on with your little finger.

Highlighter A relatively new product for extra cheek shine at night. A whipped-creamlike product that should be used as though it had as many calories—sparingly!

Fragrance

Nothing is as personal as perfume, because each scent combines with your own skin chemistry, so that none is the same on every woman who wears it. Whether you use perfume, cologne or toilet water in the fragrance of your choice depends on how much of a scent you want as an aura, the perfume being the strongest distillation and the cologne the lightest.

I would suggest perfume for evening and the other concentrations during the day. There is nothing more refreshing than a marvelous splash or spray of cologne to lift the spirits and cool the body.

Every woman should own at least two scents: one for daytime, a light, classic fragrance, and a deeper, sensuous, "important" one for evenings and dressy occasions. How many different perfumes you want to own and use is very much a matter of choice. Some women prefer to be identified with a particular scent they have made their very own, others prefer a whole galaxy of shiny bottles adorning their shelves and matching their moods.

Far better, to my way of thinking, than having a vast array of different scents is having the whole range of products available in your particular favorites.

Bath *oils*, *salts* and *foams* scent and silken the water and saturate your skin as you bathe. *Body lotions* and *powders* smoothed on after the bath continue the softening process and increase the effect of the scent on and around you. Having everything in your favorite fragrance heightens the special, pampered feeling, and, really, this is a most affordable luxury as well as a beneficial one.

A bar of *soap* in your favorite fragrance—too drying to use on your face—is good for the bath, and it also makes a perfect drawer sachet. Place cakes of soap among scarves, lingerie, hosiery, anything, for that little added touch.

Beauty Tools

Perfect application is greatly due to perfect makeup tools which assure a smooth, flawless finish. Simple, everyday products can fix little mishaps during makeup application without harming good areas.

Sponges   No other technique can give you the smoothness, the nonstreaking all-over evenness of the sponge. There is also a flexibility in the sponge that allows for more control in the *distribution* of color than the fingers alone can provide. In addition, the sponge soaks up some of the product as it applies it; thus you cannot over-apply, as you can with your fingers. And the fingers cannot give you the *uniformity* that a smooth, moving sponge can.

I would have one sponge for applying moisturizer and another for foundation and rouge. Sponges are cheap and long-lasting. In fact, I like them better as they become older. They are even more pliable and softer. Natural sponges have holes and can streak; this is one time when I prefer the artificial (foam-rubber) product to the natural one.

Brushes   Happily, most products needing a brush for application include one in the packaging. However, there are a few extra brushes that do helpful jobs: A broad sable-haired brush for loose face powder as well as for the pressed compact kind. A narrow one for powder eye shadow. (The little wand that often comes with these is not fine enough.) A lipstick brush for a professional application. A fine-tipped brush for eyeliner smudging. (The brush that comes with the liner may be too fine-tipped or not fine enough.) A brow brush (one that looks like a mini-toothbrush) for shaping and as an aid when tweezing. An eyelash brush (or comb) for easy separation of lashes and for use with cake mascara.

A *Washcloth*   Take one out of the linen closet and keep it with your skin-care products for easy removal of cleansing cream. Wet it with hot water, wring it out thoroughly and wipe away grime and makeup along with the cleanser. Always wash it out to keep it clean.

Cotton   If you use cotton balls, buy the large size. These are invaluable for applying skin lotion. For economy, buy a tremendous roll of sterile cotton and make your own pads as you need them. Here's how: pull a piece of cotton from the roll (the rest will stay clean and fresh); mold the piece under water until it's about the size and shape of a hamburger patty; shape it in your hands, tucking the edges under so it's nice and even all around. Then squeeze all the water out and apply your lotion in smooth, long strokes. Another economy: wet pads absorb less lotion than dry. For a lovely cool touch, you can make a few dozen of these cosmetic patties, moistened and drained, and then pop them into a plastic bag and store them in your refrigerator. They can also be used as eye pads, soaked in chamomile or just taken as they are, cold from the refrigerator, and placed over the eyes and forehead after you've applied a mask and have stretched out to relax as it does its work.

Cotton Swabs   These are great for getting out that last bit of mascara or eye color that sometimes hides stubbornly in the corner. But be extra careful in using anything close to the eyes.

Tissues   These are always handy to have for removing cleansing cream, for touching up a smear, for wiping your hands.

Beauty Et Ceteras

Eye Drops   Move them from the medicine cabinet to your makeup area. I like them for use after eye makeup removal and at the start of each new application.

Tweezers   For getting rid of those straggly hairs in the brows. Always follow with an astringent or alcohol application.

Eyelash Curler   A medieval-looking invention that does wonders for straight lashes—when you use it properly.

Lip Pomade   Available in stick form to keep lips nice and moist when a gloss or lipstick isn't doing that for you.

Lip Wax   For the upper lip only, to remove those dark hairs. Never wax cheeks or any other area of your face. Always use the wax on the upper lip before bedtime so that the redness can have the night hours in which to heal. (Hair can be bleached, but for the same effort, why not wax and not worry about hair for a month?)

About the Author

Pablo was born in Romagna, Italy, the son of Count and Countess Zappi-Manzoni. With a lifelong interest in beauty, he directed his talents toward the study of makeup and became Beauty Director of the Elizabeth Arden Italian salons in 1961. Elizabeth Arden brought Pablo to the United States in 1964, and in 1965 he received the Coty Fashion Award for his innovative facial designs through the artful use of cosmetics.

In addition to his work as Creative Director of Elizabeth Arden, Pablo takes great interest in and donates much time to the Industrial Home for the Blind, of which he is a vice-president, and the Irvington House.